FLY FISHING
Desert & High Arid Lakes

Steve Probasco

Frank Amato

PORTLAND

Dedication

To the women of my life—my mother, my wife and best friend, Cindy and my daughter Carly.

Carly Probasco.

All inquiries should be addressed to:
Frank Amato Publications, Inc.
P.O. Box 82112, Portland, Oregon 97282
Cover Photo: Steve Probasco
All photos by the author except where credited to another.
Fly Plates on pages 46 and 48 photographed by Jim Schollmeyer.
Book and Cover Design: Kathy Johnson

Printed in Hong Kong

1 3 5 7 9 10 8 6 4 2
ISBN: 1-57188-026-7

Lahontan cutthroat.

Contents

Dry Falls Lake, Washington desert.

A beautiful desert lake.

Foreword

The Battenkill, AuSable, Firehole, the Big Horn. Henry's Fork, Silver Creek, San Juan, the Deschutes. Alaska, Yellowstone, New Zealand, Patagonia. These rivers and places are common destinations for the fly fishing fraternity and all of these names will "ring a bell" to most fly fishers. Only our wallets dictate how far or wide we fly fishing fanatics will travel for that trophy trout, remote solitude, fog thick hatches—or, whatever it is that yanks us away; deserting family, jobs, sanity; and finds us heading off in an uncontrolled, all-out frenzy.

But, how about destinations such as Dry Falls, Pyramid, Grindstone, Quail, or Strawberry? These don't ring that bell quite so loudly you say? Probably not. Most of these waters are seldom mentioned in the fly fishing magazines, although they are all great trout waters. These waters are all true desert or high arid lakes and reservoirs; waters that are not in the limelight of the fly fishing world. But, all of these waters are close to those of us living in the west, and certainly within reach to the plethora of travelers who descend upon the more fabled trout destinations around the world. The difference—most desert and high arid lakes are loaded with gleaming, overstuffed trout that often dwarf their counterparts found in even the best of the famous rivers.

Thumb through the pages of this book and look at the pictures of some of these magnificent trout. There are desert and high arid lakes scattered across all of our western states where fishing opportunities for huge trout abound. Many anglers that I talk to are unaware of the incredible fishing that can be had in such waters. Many times, desert lakes along the route to "famous rivers" go unnoticed, with anglers oblivious to the fishing possibilities they just whizzed by.

I don't want to sound like I am bad-mouthing the great rivers or places I have mentioned. I'm not. I love fishing famous water and traveling to exotic destinations as much as any fly fisherman, and I do it often. But I am also truly obsessed with the desert and high arid lakes of the west. The finest fishing I have known has come from these lakes and reservoirs. Serenity, abundant trout, and the awesome scenery keeps me returning to the desert every chance I get.

In the pages of this book I will share with you what I have learned about desert and high arid lakes and their fish. I will cover the basic entomology of these lakes, and share the fly patterns that I use to imitate the insects and other food items found in these fertile waters. Techniques for fishing will be covered, as well as how to read the water. In short, I will tell you all I know about fishing these lakes and, if you read carefully, I might even mention some of my favorite waters.

Please be kind to the fishery. Many of our western lakes are adopting limited-kill, and no-kill regulations. Practice and promote this ethic. Catch and release works, and it is by conservation and compassion that quality fishing will remain in all of our waters. It's up to us all.

I hope this book answers some questions, sparks some interest, and sheds new light on fly fishing desert and high arid lakes. If just a fraction of my love for these lakes rubs off during your reading, you will be helplessly, hopelessly hooked—a changed person—forever searching the desert west, for a puddle in which to cast a fly.

Casting to a rising trout in the Washington desert.

Rainbow over
the hills in a
Utah desert.

Desert
rainbow.

Introduction

Many fly fishers are intimidated by the vastness of lakes, and are unsure of exactly how to approach them. This is especially true of fishermen whose trouting experience comes mostly from fishing moving water. Obviously, lakes and streams differ greatly; from their outward appearance, to the way fish respond to a host of variables, including such basics as their feeding habits. Fishing a lake is not harder than fishing a stream—it's just different. Anglers that recognize the differences and adapt their fishing skills accordingly will have few problems in the transition.

Fish in streams, for the most part, are stationary. They hold in their feeding lies waiting for food items to come with the current into their feeding position. They won't move far to take a food item, they expend as little energy as possible while feeding. Reading a stream, and recognizing where

trout hold when feeding is fairly easy when trout are feeding on insects, especially if those insects are on, or near, the surface because you can actually see the fish take the food item.

Trout in lakes must move around to find their food. Unless the fish are rising to insects, and are visible, the fisherman must rely on his or her knowledge of reading the lake in order to find the areas most likely to be holding the feeding fish at any given time. And this, I think, is where many would-be lake fishermen get scared off and, where many who are taking a stab at it, fail.

So, how do you approach a lake? Where do you start? First of all, some observation needs to be done when approaching any new water. The key word here is observation. Be observant to everything that's going on around you. I can't stress this point enough.

Before entering the water, check the shoreline for insect life. Simply looking around can tell you a lot about what is going on in the water. Are their any insects flying around? Check the water's edge for sub-aquatic life. Are there any nymphs swimming around? Scuds? Or how about leeches? What size are the nymphs, scuds or leeches? What color are they? I think you get the picture. Find out as much about the water that you can before you enter it.

Maybe there will be other fishermen that you can talk with that can share some "lake secrets" that they have gained from experience. When fishing new water, don't

A secret lake? No, but one you need to walk a ways to get to. Washington desert.

A desert rainbow.

Minnie Lake, B.C.

be afraid to ask an angler that's yanking in fish right and left just what it is that he is doing that you're not. A person who fishes any piece of water on a regular basis will have a wealth of information and is usually willing to share some of it if approached in the right way.

While you are doing your observing, check out the physical aspects of the lake before you start fishing. Do cliffs or rock walls enter the water? Are their large areas of sunken weed beds visible? How about cattails, or reeds along a shoreline? All of these physical observations will help you decide where to start, and what to start with. Put your plan of attack together while still on shore.

Once you have entered the water don't stop observing. Keep an open mind to all that you see. Hatches or feeding frenzies can start at any time, and you need to be ready to change tactics at a moment's notice. A fair knowledge of lake entomology is helpful for sure, but most important is

that you just keep your eyes open to everything around you.

Fish movements and activity in any lake is dictated by a number of factors. Water temperature, insect hatches, and the weather are but a few of the reasons trout will move around in the lake. These factors vary throughout the season, and from lake to lake. The worst thing that you can do when fishing any lake is to get hung up on tactics or flies that produced "last week" or at a lake just down the road, but aren't working on the lake you are presently fishing. What works changes daily, sometimes hourly, and I will say this just this one last time. Be observant! This is your key to success.

Lake Characteristics

High arid and desert lakes may be natural bodies of water or man-made impoundments; most often the result of water diversion and storage for agricultural purposes. Whether natural, or man-made, many of these lakes are rich in aquatic life and have become good trout fisheries.

The seep lakes region of central Washington is a prime example of true desert lakes that evolved from the agricultural diversion of water. O'Sullivan Dam was built in the early 1950s in the desert south of the town of Moses Lake, as part of an irrigation project to bring life to the sands of this barren desert. The reservoir behind the dam, known as Potholes Reservoir, grew large and the downward pressure that it created caused water to rise into many of the small canyons and valleys just south of the reservoir and extending out many miles. This area is part of the great Columbia Plateau, volcanic in origin, and it has many natural fissures and channels through which the underground water travels. Here and there the water popped to the surface as a lake. Today the area is called the "seep lakes" region, and contains more than 70 lakes, many of which contain trout.

There are desert and high arid lakes from the eastern slopes of the Cascade Mountains, and stretching out across the dry areas of most of the western states and corresponding parts of southern Canada. The numbers of these lakes is overwhelming and nearly all of them contain fish. The warm summer sun found over this part of the country is very conducive to the whole ecosystem; sub-aquatic plant growth, thus prolific insects, and—big fat trout!

There are several general characteristics and structures found in most desert and high arid lakes. Understanding these characteristics and structures can be invaluable in your quest for trout.

Shallows

Fishing shallow sections can be some of the most exciting fly fishing to be found on the desert or high arid lakes. You will often be able to stalk individual feeding fish, and follow their movement with your casts. If the lake bottom is light in color, such as that of sand, this is a particularly easy thing to do. Casting to cruisers in the shallows will get your adrenaline pumping for sure.

Lahontan cutthroat trout preparing to spawn.

Floating lines are all that's needed in the shallows. Sometimes long leaders of 15 feet or more are needed for these wary trout. Tippets of 5 or 6 feet, tapered to 6X, are not uncommon. The best way to present a fly to these fish is to observe the feeding fish for awhile and identify their route of travel. Make your cast so that your fly touches down five or six feet ahead of the fish to avoid spooking it. If you are using a nymph, keep a close eye on your leader track and set the hook as soon as there is a visible disturbance.

The shallows are best fished during the spring before the aquatic weed growth begins, as later on in the season the weeds might completely cover the area. The water temperatures will be down in the spring also, and you will often find heavy concentrations of fish packed into a relatively small area. Fish can be very selective in shallow water situations. The exact imitation of whatever food item the trout is eating is often called for in this kind of water. During the spring and early summer months in most of our lakes, midges are usually the insect that is most prevalent. Pay very close attention to the size and color of the naturals.

During the hot summer months some shallows will still be open and free of weeds. However, water temperatures will keep trout from these areas except during low light periods of the day when water temperatures are at their lowest. On the hottest of days, fishing during the night may be the only time you can take fish from this type of water.

Weed Beds

Weed beds are a virtual insect smorgasbord for trout. Aquatic vegetation attracts aquatic insects and other food items of the trout. Damselfly nymphs, dragonfly nymphs, scuds, snails; virtually all aquatic insects can be found living in weed beds. So, naturally, if you find a section of a lake with heavy aquatic vegetation, chances are you will find a concentration of fish feeding there also. Trout will cruise through the sub-aquatic jungle, often feeding unselectively on any food item that is available.

Weed beds are generally a good place to start your fishing when approaching any lake. Since we know that there will most likely be feeding fish there, this only makes sense. Positioning yourself on an outer edge of a weed bed, keeping just within casting range, is generally where you want to begin if at all possible. By doing so, you can fish the edges of the weeds and the adjacent deeper water before actually going into the weeds and risking spooking the fish. Trout will often hang out in the deeper water right next to a weed bed, consequently, this water needs to be covered very carefully.

When fishing this water adjacent to the weed bed trout will probably be found near the bottom. Unless there is a hatch or

Fishing a Washington state desert lake.

Lahontan cutthroat on a spawning mission.

Fishing the
shallows from
a Tote 'N
Float, a craft
ideal for fish-
ing shallow
water.

Desert brown trout.

Dragonfly nymphs—meat-and-potatoes for desert trout.

Adult damselflies.

Pockets in the weeds are prime spots to look for feeding trout.

Dusty Lake, Washington desert.

insect migration in progress, your flies will be most effective when fished right near the bottom. Since weed beds are shallow water structure, an intermediate or sinking-tip line will accomplish this in most situations.

After fishing the edges of the weed bed, slowly work your way in closer to the weeds, casting right into the aquatic jungle. If water depth above the weeds is sufficient, a fly worked just above the tops is in ideal position for trout cruising near the tops of the weed bed. An intermediate line is the best line for this type of fishing. Even if you need to sink down a bit further and work your fly right through the bed, the intermediate line will suffice if you simply wait a little longer before starting your retrieve.

One problem with fishing weed beds, obviously, is that you hang up often. That's just part of the game though, and your fly is where the fish are—it's just something you have to live with! Just remember to check your fly often for salad. Trout hate salad! Some fly designs work better in the weeds than others. Patterns tied on keel hooks will swim through nearly weedless.

Another problem with fishing weed beds is that when you hook a fish, especially a large one, it often heads for the bottom and security of the vegetation. Not only is the fish often lost because it tangled your leader and line in the weeds, but there is great risk of the fish dying if it is unable to free itself from your leader and the entanglement. When you hook a big fish in a weed bed, a tight reign is called for. If at all possible, try to lead it out into deeper water to finish the battle. Not only will you have a better chance of landing the fish and it surviving, but you will not stir up the weed bed and spook other feeding fish.

Cattails and Reeds

Cattails and reeds act very much like other aquatic vegetation in that the underwater portions provide insect habitat. Trout are very much in tune to this and at times will hang out just on the edge of the underwater stalks picking off the insects that thrive there. An example would be during the damselfly hatch, when nymphs swim towards shore, grasp the underwater stalks and crawl up out of the water to hatch into their adult stage of life. Trout go nuts when this happens, and fishing in tight against the reeds or cattails is a good bet.

When fishing in close to cattails or reeds I like to anchor as close to the stalks as possible. With an intermediate line, I will cast parallel to the stalks and retrieve my fly slowly, only inches from the underwater stalks.

Besides hosting a variety of aquatic insects below the surface, the above-water stalks of reeds or cattails may be crawling with terrestrial insects whose misfortune finds them fish food. At times, especially during gusty winds, ants, beetles, hoppers and other terrestrial patterns fished in tight against the stalks can produce some exciting action.

Transition Water

In lakes that have both shallow sections and deeper sections, there is usually a transition section, that is, an area where the two meet. During the spring and fall, fish may stay in the shallows and feed all day long. During the heat of summer, however, fish will often migrate from the shallows to deeper water as the sun rises, and back to feed in the shallows as the sun sinks low in the sky. During these periods, a transition zone is a good place to work your flies to the migrating trout. You can often sit in one position and have a continuous supply of trout passing by.

Tubers on
Dry Falls Lake, Washington.

The bottom structure of the transition zone may be such that the area contains fish all the time. There could be good weed growth, rocks, or other bottom habitat conducive to insects and trout. When entering a lake for the first time I will nearly always seek out a transition zone if one is available. Search patterns such as a Gold Ribbed Hare's Ear Nymph, and other nymphs that generally emulate several aquatic insects, fished on a sink-tip, or intermediate line are my usual choices for this kind of water.

Rocky Shorelines

Rocky shorelines are another area, when they are present, that deserve much attention. Just as weed beds attract aquatic insects, a rocky shoreline that extends out into the lake will attract insects and other food items as well. Small fishes, such as chubs and sculpins might be found around a rocky shoreline which attracts, of course, trout. Many times, some of the largest fish in the lake will be found around rocky shorelines feasting on baitfish and crayfish which like these areas.

Sometimes a rocky shoreline will signify the deepest areas in the lake, especially if the shoreline is at a steep angle where it enters the water. What this means is that during the heat of summer, this deeper water will provide a retreat for trout from the desert heat that has excessively warmed the shallows. There might even be a significant drop along the shoreline which is a perfect area for trout hiding out, just waiting for food to appear along the ledge. Swimming baitfish imitations or streamers along this ledge is, at times, a very rewarding tactic.

Getting your fly down to the fish and working it so that it emulates the naturals is the key, just as it is in any other type of water. A wet-tip or full-sinking line is usually called for. A good way to fish a ledge is to sit along the ledge in your boat or tube and cast parallel along the drop so that your fly is just on the "deep" side of the ledge. Another effective way to fish a drop is by simply trolling your fly along the ledge using a full-sinking line.

Cliffs and Deep Water

Cliffs that drop vertically into a lake may continue below the surface for some distance, and are usually associated with deep water. Good examples of this would be areas such as the lakes found in volcanic formed areas around the west. Immense columns of basalt can be found is such areas. In many lakes these columnar spires rise from the water and tower high above the lakes.

Fishing in the shadow of these cliffs and spires is often productive when the sun has slowed the action on the main body of the lake, especially in mid-summer when the surface water temperatures are very warm. It's always more productive to fish in these shaded areas when possible, especially for fish feeding on, or near the surface.

During the heat of the day when summer temperatures excessively warm the water near the surface, fishing right along the bottom may be the only place you can find fish, as they will be enjoying the cooler water found there. Deeper areas, usually associated with cliffs, are a good place to "dredge" on those hot, sunny days.

Fish are often lethargic under such conditions. A very slow and perceptive approach is required. With a full-sinking line, let your fly sink to the bottom. A black leech pattern or a black Woolly Bugger is a good fly for this type of fishing. Once your fly has had a chance to settle, start an extremely slow retrieve. The pick-up is often subtle, and takes may go unnoticed unless you are on your toes. You need to strike at the slightest hesitation in your fly's movement. Sometimes a take will feel exactly like your fly ticking a weed, so it is important that anytime you feel something out of the ordinary you raise your rod tip. The worst that can happen is that you will snag some weeds or the bottom. But just as often, you will be rewarded with a fish.

Many people prefer to troll their fly through deeper sections during the summer months. This is a very effective way to cover a lot of water on those particularly slow days. Using a full-sinking line, begin a slow troll. Again, the key here is moving slow.

When you hook a fish, pay particular attention to where your fly was when the fish hit, and work the area over well. There may be underwater springs in the area, and the cooler water from these will draw trout like a magnet. Again, a leech imitation is a hard pattern to beat.

Equipment & Tackle

I don't want to dwell too much on the equipment and tackle needed to fish desert and high arid lakes. I can only assume that most fly fishermen reading this book already have fly tackle, and any tackle already in possession will work fine for fishing lakes. There are, however, new and exciting lines, rods and other equipment showing up on the market that make fishing lakes a whole lot easier. As of the writing of this book, I will share with you my favorite, and most used gear when I am fishing the desert lakes.

Rods and Reels

You can get by with almost any fly rod when fishing most lakes. Casts are seldom long, and the rod you use is largely personal choice. I like rods that are 10-feet in length, and of a fairly fast action. The long rod makes casting from a tube a lot easier, and the fast action construction will make casting in the wind much easier.

Most of the time I use a 5-weight rod because of the versatility it allows, but there are times when using a small rod, such as a 2 or 3-weight is a blast. An example would be when there are heavy hatches of midges on calm days.

Sometimes I carry both rods with me when tubing, but there really isn't a good system for carrying a spare on a float tube. More often, I just carry one rod and spare spools for my reel, loaded with a few different lines.

As far as reels go, there's not much to say. Any fly reel that you have will work fine for lake fishing.

Lines

The days of poorly balanced, inefficient fly lines are long gone. There are fly lines today that effectively fish from top to bottom, regardless of the water fished, or the species you are after. Lines for fishing desert and high arid lakes are no exception.

To cover all the situations that you will encounter when fishing lakes you need to have a few different fly lines. Sure, you could get by with just one line, and if I had to recommend one line to cover most situations you will run into on the typical lake that one line would be a sinking-tip line of medium density. However, by just using one line your options would be limited.

To cover all of the depths and fishing situations you will encounter, you need a full-floating, intermediate, sink-tip and a full-sinking line. I prefer weight-forward lines for ease of casting and distance.

Most line manufacturers are now making no-stretch lines that sink at the same rate throughout their length. This eliminates the "belly" common with some lines. These lines will let you detect strikes much easier, and are by far the best you can use in a lake situation.

Leaders

Leader design often means the difference between success and failure when fishing heavily fished water. Trout may become leader shy and refuse a perfect imitation of the insects they are feeding on, simply because they are spooked by the leader. I think this factor alone is the single-most overlooked reason why "the fish aren't biting."

When fishing chironomids or some of the dry patterns over heavily fished trout, leaders of 12 to 16 feet in length and tapered down to 5X or 6X are often called for. You may break more fish off with leaders such as this, but you will also get a lot more action.

Desert rainbow.

Any time you are fishing a sinking fly your leader needs to be considerably shorter than if you are fishing dry. Seldom do you need a leader with a total length over four feet long. If the leader is too long your fly will take longer to sink and tend to work its way towards the surface. Trout are not nearly as leader shy when fishing sub-surface patterns.

You do need to make sure that the tippet material you are using is fine enough to allow your fly to swim naturally. For this reason, I most always use a tippet of 3X or 4X on my sub-surface flies. I also find that limp leader material allows my fly to swim and undulate better.

Other Gear

When fishing from a float tube or small boat you are limited to the amount of gear you can bring along, but then, you don't re- ally need much gear either. I nearly always take a net along, which makes it easier to land and quickly release large trout. If used, nets should always be the type with soft nylon bags that don't harm the fish.

The other handful of gear that I religiously take along with me includes; a camera stashed in a Ziploc bag, flashlight (I almost always fish into the night), nail nippers, thermometer, flex-light (for tying flies on in the dark), sunscreen, a couple boxes of flies—in other words, the same stuff you pack along in your fishing vest when fishing a stream.

Above: Collection of fly tackle.

Below: Streamer and leech box.

Food Items

One of the first steps you must take before you fish a desert or high arid lake is to familiarize yourself with the food items that are available to the trout. This is not a hard task. There just aren't that many insects or other foods that you need to know about. And, for heavens sake, you don't need to know everything about the insects and other trout foods to get started.

You must know some basics though; what each insect or other food item looks like—both the underwater and above water stage for those that have both. You need to know where the sub-aquatic foods are likely to be found because that's where the fish will be. And, you need to have an understanding of how these food items appear to fish in the water, how they move, and when they will be present in numbers to entice feeding trout.

Once you are aware of some of these "food" basics, you will be able to locate, and catch trout in lakes. In this chapter, I go over the most important insects and food items found in our desert and high arid lakes. I will also share with you some of the flies that I use to imitate these insects, and how to fish them.

Waterboatman
(Order: Hemiptera, Family: Corixidae)

The waterboatman and the backswimmer are the two most important aquatic members (to the fly fisherman) of the order Hemiptera. Since for all practicality, they look and act very much alike, I will address them both as "boatmen."

Waterboatmen are, at times, very important to the lake fly fisherman, especially during the spring and fall months. Many anglers fail to realize the importance of the boatman, and miss out on the action during the select times when trout are tuned into them. Although not as important in the trout's diet as many of the aquatic insects, the wise angler will have a few imitations of the boatman in his fly box.

Waterboatmen are easily identified by watching them swim. They have three pairs of legs. The front two pairs are small and insignificant, but their hind legs are large and oar shaped, and propel them through the water in a fast and very erratic fashion. Waterboatmen are short, stalky looking bugs. They eat small aquatic insects such as midge larvae. Some species of the boatman grow to nearly one-half-inch long, but most are considerably smaller. Their backs are an olive-brown color in most waters, with a lighter underside.

Waterboatmen must surface to collect oxygen. They trap an air bubble on the underside of their abdomen, and return back down to the bottom where they can survive for long periods before surfacing again. Since they must make frequent trips to the sur-

Desert lake fly box full of small nymphs.

face, boatmen are seldom found in water deeper than five feet. At rest, the boatmen float in the surface film, head down.

Imitations of the boatman can be fished from top to bottom. When trout are chowing on resting adults, a greased line approach can be very effective. Grease your leader with fly floatant—all but the last inch or so from your fly. With a floating line and greased leader, your boatman imitation will hang in the film just like the natural. If trout are taking these insects below the surface, a wet-tip line approach is in order. Cast out, and let your fly sink to the bottom. With a very erratic stripping motion draw your line in. If trout are feeding on boatmen, expect a violent take.

My favorite boatman pattern is tied with a body of Spirit River's flash dubbing, which has a sparkle that emulates the air bubble on the natural. For the wings, I use turkey quill tied shell-back. For the legs, a turkey quill fiber is tied so that it sticks out of each side of the body. I then use Dave's Flexament on the shell-back and legs for durability.

Caddisflies
(Order: Trichoptera)

There are roughly one thousand species of caddis that have been identified in the waters of the United States and Canada. They are second in abundance only to the innumerable species of Diptera. Trichoptera have a complete metamorphosis of egg, larvae, pupa and adult. This life cycle usually takes about one year to complete, but there is a variance in each direction. Size of this insect varies greatly, from the microcaddis which are about three millimeters in length, to the giant, two-inch caddisflies such as those found in the interior lakes of British Columbia. They are customarily called "sedges" in that province.

Caddisflies are widespread, and are found in most desert and high arid lakes. In some lakes however, caddis are much more prolific than in others. A knowledge of local entomology will certainly help when exploring lakes in any given area. I have fished lakes where hatches of caddisflies were very insignificant, and others close-by where evening hatches filled the air with the erratically flying adults. It is wise when fishing any lake to have an assortment of caddis in the larval, pupal and adult stages; the pupal being the most important.

Larvae

Caddis larvae are segmented and worm-like in appearance, with six jointed legs protruding from near their head. There are two main types of caddis larvae that inhabit lakes; the case builders, and the free swimmers.

Case builders are recognized by everyone; periwinkles, as they are often called. These caddis build protective cases around themselves out of any debris they can find, such as pebbles, sand, small sticks and tiny pieces of vegetation. They bond

these materials together with a sticky material secreted from their salivary glands. Larvae sizes range to nearly one-and-one-half inches in length. Colors range from grays, to greens, to creams, to browns and orange. Case builders pull themselves along the lake bottom and over obstacles with their long legs, in search of food items which consist largely of immature insects and algae.

Imitations of the cased caddis should be fished right along the bottom. A full-sinking, or wet-tip line is used, and the fly is allowed to sink down to the bottom. Since cased caddis move so slowly, let the movement created by the breeze or slight movements of your rod do all the working of the fly for you. Although not extremely important to the lake fly fisher, fishing the cased caddis can be productive at times, and so it's worth carrying a few imitations in your box.

A simple pattern that I use is tied on a weighted Daiichi 1270 hook, ranging from size 10 through 22, depending on the size of the naturals available. It consists of a natural burlap body, and a head of black ostrich herl palmered with a couple turns of black hen hackle.

Stillwater caddis imitation.

The free swimmers don't build cases, but swim around, sheltering themselves by hiding around vegetation. They are found in the shallow sections of a lake with good light penetration. Free swimmer imitations are fished in and around vegetation. Use an intermediate, or wet-tip line to place your fly into the cover. As with the cased version, let the natural currents or slight movement of your rod work the fly, and be ready for subtle takes.

A simple, free swimming caddis larvae can be imitated with a dubbed body of your favorite dubbing (color to match the naturals) and a head of black ostrich herl.

Pupae

When the caddis larvae matures, it pupates. Case builders seal the entrance to their cases, and the free swimmers build silken cocoons. The pupal body forms inside the case, and as it matures, the adult caddis forms inside the pupal husk. Emergence can take place spring through fall, but the heaviest emergence is during the spring and early summer months in most desert and arid lakes. When the pupae swims to the surface, it does so slowly and it is this stage of the caddis that is the most vulnerable to feeding trout. When caddis adults are observed on the water, fishing a caddis pupae properly may be just the ticket.

A good pattern to use during the emergence is a soft hackle, tied with a body of Antron dubbing or Sparkle Yarn. These body materials trap air, and when drawn to the surface they look very much like the ascending caddis pupae. Another fly that works well during the emergence is a pupae consisting of an Antron dubbed body, a black ostrich herl head, and a partridge hackle wound a couple of turns between the body and head. You should tie this fly in several earth-tone colors to match a variety of naturals.

The caddis pupae can be fished in a variety of waters. Depending on depth, fish it one of two ways. In medium to fairly deep water, use a full-sinking or sinking-tip line. Let your fly sink to the bottom and then slowly draw your pupae imitation to the surface. If trout are feeding on the pupae, you will quickly find out. If the water is fairly shallow, make your cast using an intermediate or full-floating line and let your fly sink to just under the surface. Trout often take the emerging pupae there, and your pattern will be a sitting duck to trout feeding on, or near, the surface. Let the breeze or slight movement of your rod-tip make your imitation move ever-so-slightly. Takes can be violent, but they can also be subtle, so be on your toes.

Adult

As the pupae ascends to the surface, the pupal husk splits down the back and the adult struggles out, often right in the surface film. Some caddis fly right out of their husks as they reach the surface. Many of the large caddisflies need to sit on their pupal husk and dry their wings before they can become airborne. This is a very perilous time for the adults. Trout pick them off, seemingly with a vengeance, creating big, splashy rises. The angler who witnesses such an occurrence will have a heyday if he has some adult caddis imitations in his fly box.

The adult caddis has two sets of wings that are one-and-one-half to two times the length of its body. At rest, the caddis holds its wings parallel to its body in an inverted V fashion. The wing looks like a little pup-tent sitting on the back of the caddis. It has long antennae curving over its back, and long legs. The adult looks very much like a moth in flight, but at close observation there is no mistaking the two.

During a heavy hatch, an Elk Hair Caddis in the appropriate size cast out amongst the rises may be all that's needed. A big adult trying to struggle free of its pupal husk causes quite a disturbance on the water. Twitching your fly to resemble the naturals may trigger more strikes than just letting your fly sit motionless.

If the hatch is not real heavy, or if the water is extremely flat, you may need to use a more realistic looking imitation. My favorite fly for these situations is a Quill Wing Caddis. Tied with a dubbed body, turkey quill wing, and a hackle trimmed top and bottom, this fly rides low on the water and looks very realistic.

Damselflies (Order: Odonata)

The order Odonata is the oldest order of all insects. Damselflies, (sub-order: Zygoptera) are very common in desert waters across the west, and in North America there are over one hundred known species. Many make the mistake and call damselflies "dragonflies." Although there are some similarities, they are completely different insects. The outright difference is size. Damselflies, both nymphs and adults, are much smaller than dragonflies. However, damselflies are still a sizable morsel, and are a major entree in the trout's diet.

Damselfly nymphs.

Damselflies go through an incomplete metamorphosis of egg, larvae, and adult, excluding the pupal stage. It is the larval (nymph) stage of the damselfly that is of the most concern to the lake fisherman.

Damselfly nymphs can be easily identified. They have a long, slender, segmented abdomen with what appears to be three paddle-shaped tails, but in actuality are the nymph's gills. They have six legs attached to the thorax, and large eyes that are set widely apart. The nymphs are usually shades of olives and browns, and are lighter in color on the ventral (underside) surface. Damselflies go through several molts during their life until they reach maturity, and sometimes reach a length of one-and-one-half inches.

Damselflies live in and around aquatic vegetation and can be fished with imitations in these areas year-round. But perhaps the best time to fish a damsel imitation is during their emergence, which, generally speaking, occurs in late spring to early summer in most of the desert and high arid lakes around the west. When the nymphs mature, they swim towards shore with an undulating movement, making frequent rest stops. As the nymphs make this journey they are easy targets to feeding trout and, in fact, at times create an all-out feeding frenzy, with trout wildly slamming the nymphs just under the surface. An intermediate sinking line, long finely tapered leader, and a damselfly nymph imitation worked slowly near the surface, or around shoreline vegetation is deadly during the emergence.

Damselfly nymphs crawl out of the water onto any structure that will allow them to do so. At the shoreline this may be reed stocks, cattails, or whatever it is that makes up the perimeter of the lake. Damsels are not picky about what they crawl out on, and during the emergence you may find them crawling up your float tube, boat, waders or anything else that rises from the water.

After the nymphs are out of the water they cling to whatever it was they crawled out on, and wait for their nymphal shuck to split along the back and, as if by magic, the adult damselfly appears. The adult waits for its wings to dry and then flies away.

Adult damselflies are a common sight around the lakes and reservoirs throughout the spring and summer. Most common to the desert west are damsels of the genus Enallagma which are bright blue and black. Males are more intensely colored than the females. Adult damselflies have two pairs of wings and are very graceful, extremely fast fliers that seem to appear and disappear at the blink of an eye.

Adult damsels are not as important to the fly fisher as the nymphs, but they still have their place, and all lake anglers should have a few adult patterns in their fly box. Trout rise to the spent adults at times, and on breezy days will nearly always be on the alert for adults blown onto the water.

I remember one windy day in particular, while fishing a desert lake in eastern Washington. I was sitting in my float tube watching adult damsels being blown off of reed stocks into the water. With each gust, the damsels would hit the water and, there to meet them were hungry trout, "in tune" with the action. I, too, cleaned up on the action as my adult imitation was taken eagerly by the concentration of fish. I have seen this type of activity a few times since, and when trout are onto the adult damsels, anglers with adult imitations are usually well rewarded.

Dragonfly Nymph (Order: Odonata)

The dragonfly nymph is one of the largest aquatic food items found in the lakes and reservoirs around the west, or anywhere for that matter. These nymphs range in size up to two inches in length. Believe me, trout aren't oblivious to a morsel of that size. The dragonfly nymph can fall prey to trout during every month of the year, but is most vulnerable during the emergence, which will take place from May through August, depending on weather and water conditions.

Dragonfly nymphs are scary looking little creatures that live from one to four years. They are ruthless predators that attack any insect or minnow fry small enough for them to grasp. Like the

Dragonfly nymph.

damselflies, dragonfly nymphs have an extendible labium (lower lip) which allows them to swiftly grab an unsuspecting lunch from a distance.

Dragonfly nymphs have a flattened abdomen that is wider than the thorax and head. They have six legs and large beady eyes. Their gills are internal and located in the rectal chamber. The nymph is jet-propelled by forcing water out of this chamber. Colors range from dark grays to chocolate brown in the mud and bottom dwellers, to light browns, greens and yellows in the weed dwellers. Weed dwelling nymphs have more slender and longer bodies than the squat, mud dwellers.

At the time of emergence, nymphs crawl out of the water onto the shoreline vegetation; rocks, roots, etc. There they wait for the sun to dry their case, and then split behind the head and the adult appears. It takes some time for the wings of the adult to dry before it can fly off. Adult dragonflies are huge, with wingspans of up to six inches. Like the adult damselflies, adult dragonflies have two sets of wings and are incredibly graceful fliers. The adults are of little importance to the fly fisher.

When the nymphs are emerging, an imitation cast out over weed beds and slowly stripped, in four to six inch jerks, can be deadly. Trout taking emerging nymphs are on a mission and can provide some fast action to the angler with a few dragonfly nymphs in his box.

Some fly patterns used to imitate the nymph of the dragonfly include; the Carey Special (with green, black or brown chenille body), the Doc Spratley, or more realistic ties like those found in local fly shops or mail-order catalogs.

My favorite dragonfly nymph is a simple, yet realistic tie. It consists of a dark olive body, natural brown hen hackle for the legs, and monofilament eyes. Useful patterns should be tied in sizes 4 to 10, 3X to 4X long.

Mayflies (Order: Ephemeroptera)

There are over six hundred species of mayflies in North America. All trout are tuned into the hatches of these prolific insects, both the nymphal and adult stages. The most abundant, and thus the most important, mayfly species to the desert lake fisherman is the *Callibaetis*. At times, *Callibaetis* will steal the show, and exact imitations of this insect, either the nymphal or adult stage, are all that work.

Metamorphosis of the mayfly is incomplete. It goes from egg to nymph, and then to adult. Most of the mayfly's life is spent in the nymphal form, where the nymph molts (sheds its skin) several times as the nymph grows. When the adult mayfly leaves the nymphal case it is called a dun, only to shed another skin before it reaches its final adult stage known as a spinner.

Nymphs

Mayfly nymphs may be identified as follows. The nymph has a head, thorax and an abdomen. The head has a pair of large eyes and a pair of short antennae. The thorax is formed of three segments, with one pair of legs on each segment. Wing pads will be visible on the middle segment. The abdomen consists of ten segments. The nymph will have two or three tails. Gills are along the sides of the abdomen, which distinguish the mayfly nymph from other nymphs.

Callibaetis mayfly nymphs are found in heavily-vegetated areas of a lake. When the nymph is mature, it swims to the surface to hatch. It is very vulnerable to feeding trout at this time. Flies such as the Gold Ribbed Hare's Ear Nymph or the Timberline Emerger, in the appropriate size, are excellent during this emerging stage. With a full-sinking, or sinking-tip line (depending on water depth) cast your fly out and let it settle. Start a slow, steady retrieve and be ready for subtle takes.

At times, the trout might be taking emerging nymphs right near the surface, and look to the angler like they are feeding on the adults. Sometimes you must fish your nymph with a floating line, just under the surface. Often, no, or very slight, movement of your fly is the best tactic for these fish.

Duns

After the *Callibaetis* nymph has made it to the surface, the thorax splits along the top and the adult appears. The dun is drab, brownish-olive in color, with mottled wings. It now sits in the surface film and waits for its wings to harden and dry before it can take flight. The wings sit upright and look just like a tiny sailboat. This insect is again very vulnerable at this period and it is this period of the mayfly's existence where the dry fly enthusiast can have a heyday. Trout often go nuts on the adults during this period.

Callibaetis mayfly dun.

Hatches of the dun mayfly are pretty predictable. Since they are controlled by factors such as water temperature and weather, they usually happen at about the same time each year in any given piece of water. Generally speaking, the hatches happen during the most pleasant part of the day. In spring, this would be during mid-afternoon, early morning and late evening during the heat of summer, and again in mid-afternoon as fall rolls around.

A fly that works very well for imitating the *Callibaetis* is the Adams. Parachute style flies work best in still waters, and your flies should exactly match the size of the adults. If the Adams gets refusals, try the same style of fly with a body color that more exactly matches that of the natural. A dead drifting fly, using a floating line and long, fine leader is important for this type of fishing.

Spinners

Mayflies are the only insect with two winged adult stages. The spinner has a shiny body and clearer wings than the dun. It has larger eyes, larger forelegs and a longer tail. After the dun leaves the water it flies to shore and will cling to vegetation for up to several days depending on the species and the weather. When the time is right, the skin of the dun splits and out pops the mature, reproductive stage; the spinner.

The males fly over the water in swarms and the females fly into the ball of males, choose a mate and copulate. The males then die. Some species of mayflies drop their eggs from the air, some

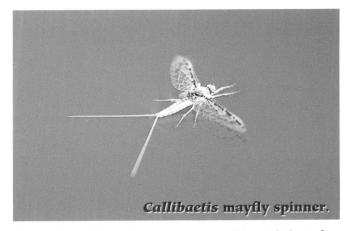

Callibaetis mayfly spinner.

deposit them right on the water, some crawl beneath the surface to lay eggs on underwater structure.

The *Callibaetis* females return to resting spots along the shore until the eggs are ready to hatch, which is around five days. The female spinners then oviposit by dipping their abdomen under the water and releasing their eggs. The eggs then hatch almost immediately and begin the cycle all over again.

After the female lays her eggs, she also dies. In some species of mayflies females fall to the surface of the water and their wings lay flat on the surface (spent spinner). Sometimes trout feed voraciously on this stage of the mayfly and you should have spinner patterns to match several different size and body colors of spent mayfly spinners, although spent *Callibaetis* spinners are seldom of significance to the desert lake fisherman.

My favorite spent spinner pattern is a small fly with a dubbed body, two deer hairs separated for the tail, and a wing of white polypropylene, tied to the side to imitate the horizontal wings of the natural spent spinner.

Midges (Order: Diptera)

The order Diptera includes such insects as mosquitoes, houseflies, no-see-ums, black flies, craneflies, and countless numbers of midges. The most important of the Dipterans to the fly fisher is the Chironomidae midge. The chironomid is found in all types of water, and is a mainstay in the diet of stillwater trout. These tiny insects are incredibly abundant. Although many species are minute, their teeming population makes them a major food source to trout, and are available every month of the year.

The Chironomidae go through a complete metamorphosis in their life cycle of egg, larvae, pupae, and adult. It is the pupal stage of the chironomid that is most vulnerable to feeding trout. However, the fly fisher should go prepared with imitations of the larvae, pupae and adult, when fishing stillwaters. At times, having just the right stage of chironomid can be your ticket to success.

Larvae

Chironomid larvae are worm-like in appearance, and are found mostly along lake bottoms of mud, algae, or silt, although there are some species that are free-swimming, and some that build small cases. The larval stage of the chironomid lasts from only a few weeks in some waters, to well over a year in others. However, most require less than a year to mature. Larvae will range in size from very tiny worms, up to an inch in length. Chironomid larvae are found in many colors. Water ph seems to play a major role in the colors of larvae. Alkaline waters with plenty of dissolved oxygen will contain larvae in shades of browns, blacks, and greens. Bright red, red-brown, and maroon colored larvae come from waters with less oxygen. They are usually found in the bottom mud and are called bloodworms. Their color is due to hemoglobin in their blood.

Fishing chironomid larvae on the bottom requires much patience and extreme concentration. Adjust your tackle (line and leader combination) so that your fly will quickly sink to the bottom. Very slowly, raise and lower your rod tip so that the fly dances over the muck. The key here is to work your fly slowly. Be prepared for a pause or very light take as the trout sucks in your fly. Another excellent technique for fishing chironomid larvae is to "dead drift" out of a boat or tube. Using a full-floating or wet-tip line (depending on water depth) cast out and simply drift with the wind, or very slowly kick along if there is no wind. As with the bottom dancing, use a 4X or 5X tippet so that your larval imitation will appear as lifelike as possible. When fishing in this manner trout will take your fly as a free-swimming larvae.

The larvae may be imitated with very simple fly patterns. Small flies of nothing more than sparsely dubbed fur or other dubbing are usually all that's needed.

Pupae

Imitating the pupal stage of the chironomid is most important to the fly fisher, for it is this stage that is most important to trout. When the larvae has matured, it pupates. Chironomid pupae have thin segmented abdomens, thick thoraxes with obvious wing pads, and tufted gills at the head of the thorax. Colors range in shades of black, green, brown, gray, and amber. Sizes range like the larvae, from very small, to nearly an inch in length.

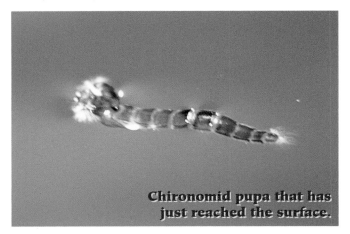

Chironomid pupa that has just reached the surface.

Chironomid pupae are free swimming. When they begin their ascent to the surface, where they hatch into the adult stage, they are very vulnerable. Chironomid pupae are slow swimmers that seemingly struggle as they inch along. They make frequent rest stops along the way. At any time during the ascent they are prime target for feeding trout, but are perhaps in the greatest peril when they reach the surface. Once in the surface film, the pupae hangs vertically while the adult struggles free of the pupal husk. Trout will cruise just beneath the surface picking off these pupae by the hundreds. As they do, they leave only a dimple on the surface. Many fishermen ignore this type of surface activity, assuming that the small rise was made by a small fish. Not so.

The chironomid pupae imitation can be fished at any depth. To fish the ascending pupae, start with your fly near the bottom. In short, intermittent surges, pull your fly ever so slowly towards the surface. You can expect a take at any time during the retrieve. If there is a breeze, a dead drift with a slight retrieve is

very productive. But, however you fish the pupae, the key is to move it slowly.

My favorite method for fishing chironomid pupae is to concentrate on the surface film. To do this, use a full floating or intermediate fly line. I prefer the latter. When greased, it rides lower in the surface film than the full-floating line, and isn't affected by wind nearly as bad. Either line will work. The method goes like this: Grease your leader (12 feet to 15 feet tapered to 4X or 5X) to within two inches of your fly. Cast out into an area where fish are working and let your fly sit motionless. Keep a keen eye on your floating leader. When your leader dips down sharply, raise your rod tip, as a trout has sipped in your fly. If you don't set the hook when your leader dips, the fish will often spit your fly out without so much as a bump detected.

At times trout will be feeding on the chironomid pupae well down below the surface. Since chironomid pupae are available to trout most of the time, this will usually be the case, if they aren't taking them on the surface. A method that works well under these circumstances is a long leader and weighted fly. The fly is weighted during the tying process with lead wire. Place a strike indicator on your leader 5 feet to 10 feet above your fly, depending on water depth, and the depth you want to fish. Grease your leader above the indicator. The leader from your indicator to the fly will sink, and the strike indicator will act like a miniature bobber, which it is. Now, simply watch your indicator. When it moves, or goes down, set the hook. At times, when trout are picky, this is often the most effective method you can use. I have found this to be especially true during the mid-day doldrums when nothing much is happening.

My favorite pupal imitation is a variation of the TDC, a very popular chironomid pupae pattern. This fly may be tied in any appropriate color to match the naturals, but I have found black to be the most productive under most situations. The fly consists of an abdomen of black floss, V-Rib, Flexi-Floss, or whatever material you prefer, ribbed with silver wire or white thread. The thorax is dubbed Antron or any other dubbing in the appropriate color, a wing case of black Swiss Straw, and gills of white poly yarn.

Adults

The adult chironomid looks much like a mosquito. Fortunately, they don't bite. The adults are usually airborne before they become trout food, but occasionally are taken on the surface while they dry their wings.

Adult chironomids are dull in color and range from blacks, to greens, to tans. Some adults can be as long as one inch in length. The wings of the adult chironomid are transparent, and they hold them flat over their back while at rest.

Fishing an adult imitation is very much like fishing the pupae. Using a long, fine leader, cast out into an area where trout are working. If you can spot your tiny fly, simply watch for the take. If you can't distinguish your imitation from the naturals on the water, watch your leader, and set the hook just as you would while fishing the pupae.

The best fly I have found for imitating the adult midge is a simple pattern which consists of a sparse hackle tail, tying thread or sparsely dubbed body, and a few turns of quality dry fly hackle at the head. Black components are my favorite, but sometimes an olive or tan midge adult saves the day.

Sometimes trout key in on the emergent stage, that is, the adult trying to wiggle free from the pupal husk. When this is the case, the Griffith's Gnat is probably the best pattern you can use. This is a pattern developed by George Griffith, and consists of a

body wound of peacock herl, palmered with a grizzly hackle. In Ernest Schwiebert's book, *Nymphs,* he recommends trimming the hackle off the top and bottom of the fly so that it floats flush in the film, for very picky fish. I do this to all my Gnats, and feel that it is a much better tie than leaving the hackle full. Size 16 is my usual choice of hook sizes. It seems that trout take this size even when larger or smaller midges are hatching. But, I also carry some smaller sizes too...just in case!

A handful of chironomids gathered from our tent rainfly after a heavy hatch.

You will find chironomids hatching every month of the year, as long as there is open water. However, the largest and most intense hatches are during the spring months. Throughout summer and fall, chironomids will hatch sporadically, but will usually be heaviest in the morning and evening hours.

Crayfish (Order: Decapoda)

If you fish lakes that contain crayfish, be certain to have some small crayfish patterns in your arsenal. Being a nocturnal crustacean, fishing the crayfish is best done in low-light hours or after dark.

Crayfish vary in color from a brownish black to brownish orange to an olive brown. Check out the colors of crayfish in the water you fish and go armed with the appropriate colors. Fish crayfish patterns with a jerky movement right along the bottom to mimic the natural. Although the crayfish is best fished under the cover of darkness, I have done very well with a crayfish fly fished deep on bright sunny days, and even in shallow water on overcast days.

Leeches (Class: Hirudinae)

Virtually all lakes contain leeches. If there is one food item you can bet that fish will respond to, in any water, at almost any given time, the leech is it. Flies that resemble this blood-sucking parasite nearly always work.

The body of the leech is long, flat on the top and bottom, and tapered at the ends. Sucker-like disks are at each end of the body, and the posterior disk is larger, and used for suction, the anterior disk is used for feeding.

Leeches may live for five years and grow very large in that amount of time. When swimming, such a leech can exceed 400 millimeters in length. Their coloration is usually shades of brown, black or olive. They may be mottled or striped, often in bright colors. Some leeches have a maroon undertone.

Leeches are common in most water and a favorite food of trout everywhere.

Leeches undulate through the water very slowly. When fishing imitations, your fly should be fished in a like manner. You want to fish them on the bottom, retrieving slowly in a pulsating fashion. Use whatever line necessary to keep your fly near the bottom, usually a full sinking line is the most practical.

I like to use a Uniform Sink Line from Scientific Anglers, or one of the new sinking lines from Airflo because of their fish detecting abilities. These lines are designed to sink evenly, eliminating the "belly" found in many sinking lines. When the line sinks at a uniform rate throughout its length, you can detect a fish as soon as it takes your fly, which will obviously increase the number of fish you land. If you have slack, or a big dip in the middle of your line, a fish will often pick your fly up and spit it out again before you have time to react.

There are many streamer fly patterns that imitate the leech. In the best imitations, marabou will be incorporated somewhere in the fly. Marabou has an undulating action in water that very closely resembles the natural movement of the leech.

Probably the most widely used pattern that resembles the leech is the Woolly Bugger. It has been said a million times (or more) by a million fly fishermen (or more) that if they only had one fly to fish with for any species, in any kind of water, or, anyplace in the world...it would be the Woolly Bugger. And I believe that's true for me also. The Woolly Bugger works magic, and I think it is largely due to the fact that the fish are taking it for one of their favorite foods—the leech. This fly has taken more big fish for me than any other fly pattern I have ever tried.

Of course, there are plenty of other patterns that resemble leeches, and many of them much more closely. For instance, a simple fly tied completely of marabou is very realistic looking when swimming through the water. Another effective way to emulate the undulating actions of the leech is with a strip-leech, tied using

Small baitfish, food for larger trout.

a piece of rabbit hide (with fur intact) tied to the hook shank Matuka-style.

My very favorite "big fish" fly that I use in waters where five to ten pound trout are common is a big strip-leech style fly tied on a size 4 hook. This fly is know by my fishing buddies as my "night leech" as I frequently use this pattern after dark to entice big browns and rainbows. It consists of a marabou tail, ESTAZ or plastic chenille body, the rabbit strip tied Matuka-style, and a ringneck pheasant rump feather tied in as a hackle. I tie it in black, brown and olive, but feel that black is the most productive under most fishing situations.

When fishing any leech pattern the fish will sometimes strike short, as they tend to first take the leech from behind. If you have a fly with a long marabou tail this is especially so. The tendancy is to strike at the first detection of a fish. If you do this you will often pull the fly away from the fish. If the fish strikes short it will often hit again more aggressively. When fishing leeches, it is best to be sure of the take before setting the hook, and most often, setting the hook isn't needed as the strike will be definite and savage.

Mice (Class: Mammalia)

I must briefly mention the importance of the mouse for those who fish during the night, especially in lakes where big browns are present. Fishing a big mouse imitation is one of the most exciting ways to fish during the night. The rise of a large trout in the darkness as it slams your mouse is an event not easily forgotten.

Mouse patterns are best fished along a rocky shoreline or along a shoreline where there is a steep bank where a mouse might naturally fall in and become trout food. When fishing a mouse pattern, use a sinking-tip line. Cast in tight along the shore, or, if it is a rocky shoreline cast your fly right into the rocks along the shore. Now, plop your fly into the water. If a big feeding brown is close by...you will know it. If nothing happens, let your fly sit a moment while waiting for the sinking-tip line to settle a bit. After your line has sunk, make a sharp, quick strip of your line. This will cause the big buoyant mouse to draw under with a "plop" mimicking a real mouse falling into the water. This commotion will often cause a feeding fish to come investigate. Try this strip several times before picking up and casting to the shore again.

When fishing a big fly like this, you need a strong tippet of around ten to fifteen pounds in order to turn the fly over. Remember, when night fishing short casts are all that's needed. It is dangerous to whip around a lot of line in the dark. Short, ten to twenty foot casts work just fine.

There are several mouse patterns that work well for night fishing. Most are tied of deer, elk or caribou hair for their bulk and buoyancy. Simple, trimmed patterns of spun deer hair and a few grizzly hackles tied in for the tail are probably the easiest to make. The Whitlock Mouse Rat is definitely the most realistic mouse pattern in existence. With a pattern like this you can't go wrong at night if big browns are present.

Scuds (Order: Amphipoda)

There are around fifty different species of scuds. They range in size from five to twenty millimeters, and come in a variety of colors. These colors range from dark green to a nearly transparent watery green. They are also found in shades of brown, red, purple and gray. The color of the scud is governed, for the most part, by its environment.

Scuds.

Scuds are a very important food item to trout. In some lakes, where scuds are prolific, they are the staple food source. Lakes with healthy scud populations grow large, deep-red fleshed trout.

Most scuds are shallow water critters, and are found in shallow vegetation or submerged debris. Wherever scuds are present, you can be sure that trout are aware of this presence and will feed aggressively on them.

Scuds are most active during the night or on dark overcast days. So, due to the nature of the crustacean, scud patterns are most productive during low light periods of early morning, late evening and on throughout the night.

There are several different scud designs available in fly shops. I find that a simple pattern of dubbed Antron, or a similar dubbing material picked loose after winding, and a shell-back of clear plastic, is about as effective as any pattern.

Snails (Class: Gastropoda)

Freshwater snails are probably the most overlooked food item in trout waters. Nearly all freshwater lakes have populations of these mollusks, and at times, they are very important when fishing the desert, or any other lake.

Snail patterns may surprise you during those times when nothing seems to work on your favorite water. All water has slow periods, and a simple snail pattern has saved my bacon more than once when such was the case.

My favorite snail pattern is a simple one shown to me by Gary Borger, it consists of a peacock herl and copper wire body, with a brown neck hackle wound fore and aft.

Fish this pattern on a floating line. Cast it out into an area where the sub-aquatic vegetation is thick and let it sink. Retrieve the fly in a slow fashion with long pauses between retrieves, letting the fly partially sink down again between strips. The retrieve of this fly is only to attract the fish, not to imitate movements of the snail.

Ant patterns.

Terrestrials

It is important to keep in mind that, at times, terrestrials such as ants, beetles, grasshoppers, crickets, bees, and a host of other land insects find themselves trout food on occasion. This is especially true on windy days when a sudden, strong gust blows the hapless insects into the water.

Flying insects and shoreline bugs all become victim from time to time. When such misfortune does happen, trout are almost always willing to take advantage of the situation. By keeping a small selection of terrestrial insects with you when fishing lakes, you can also take advantage of the situation should it occur.

Fishing a western desert lake for trout.

Presentation & Techniques

Once you have learned about the basic insects and food items found in desert and high arid lakes, and a few things about lake characteristics, most of your work is done. It is now simply a matter of presentation and technique; just how to fish your flies, and where to fish them. Although you will never stop learning new techniques and different methods of presentation, the basics are not hard to get a handle on.

Techniques vary from fisherman to fisherman—every successful angler has a system that works well for them. Just as in stream fishing, there are lake anglers who do considerably better than others. The reasons are simple—the successful fisherman pays attention to all the details, from hatches, water temperatures, weather and, in general, considers all of the factors involved. Presentation and technique is everything when it comes to fishing over snooty fish.

How you present your fly is, in my opinion, often more important than what fly you use. One of the most important points to consider about insects is that they all swim or move differently in the water. Too many people use the same techniques for fishing every fly in their box—and that's a big mistake!

Whatever fly pattern you choose to use, keep in mind what insect or other food item it emulates, or, if it is a general pattern that doesn't really imitate any one insect, consider what food item it most likely resembles and fish it appropriately.

You need to pay particular attention to how the natural insects move in the water. Most insects move slowly, with pauses in their progress. Your imitation needs to be fished in that exact manner if you are to be more than occasionally successful. The most common mistake by fishermen is to fish their flies too fast. Float tubers that simply troll their flies and never stop to work them are missing out on a lot of action, especially when the fishing is on the slow side. This is particularly true in catch-and-release water where the fish have been caught many times before. These fish certainly require your imitations to appear natural.

When working over an area where you know fish are feeding, a persistent and observant approach will most often pay off. If you can see the swirls of fish feeding just under the surface, you can catch those fish. Too many people give up after trying a few flies and, either move on, or go back to trolling. There are only three reasons why

When the fishing's hot, a double catch of browns is not uncommon.

you are unsuccessful at catching a feeding fish; either you are using the wrong fly, wrong line and/or leader for the situation, or you are imparting an unnatural movement on your fly. All three errors can be corrected.

Sometimes it is hard to tell just exactly what insect the trout are taking at the moment. This is especially true in the low-light hours when there are often multiple hatches going on. A situation that comes to mind in a favorite lake of mine happens just before dark during the summer months. The chironomids start hatching, fish are gorging themselves and, all of a sudden the strikes stop, even though the fish are still actively feeding. Close observation often reveals that the fish have taken to the adult stage of chironomid, or even a smaller midge. Making the change to another fly keeps the hook-ups coming. Too many people get locked in on what was happening, and are reluctant to change.

As far as the line/leader combination goes, obviously your fly needs to be where fish are feeding. Lines are available enabling you to do exactly that, regardless of depth. Your leader design can be critical for a couple of reasons. A fine tippet will be less visible to the fish, resulting in more strikes, especially when fishing over heavily fished trout. A fine diameter tippet will also allow for more natural movement of your fly—something that I feel is most important.

There are times when trolling a fly from a float tube can be particularly effective. When you can't locate fish feeding in the usual places by simply casting and retrieving, a slow troll in a tube will let you cover a lot of water, increasing your chances of finding willing feeders. If you resort to this type of fishing, you can increase the number of hook-ups by varying the speed of your troll, making erratic kicks with your fins or changing directions.

Here is a common scenario: You are kicking along in your tube, trolling a fly. Nothing much seems to be happening—strikes are few and not too often. You decide to grab a soda, eat a sandwich, change flies, etc., and stop your troll while fumbling around in the pockets of your tube. More than likely your tube will be rocking and twisting as you access the pockets in search for...whatever. While you are doing this, bam...fish on!

What has happened is that your fly that had been moving along at a constant pace, all of a sudden did something different. It stopped, settled, and changed directions in short little jerks as you moved around in the tube. Trout that paid little or no attention to the fly swimming along at a constant pace became interested in the fly that acted as if it were a real, pulsating something to eat.

Although, as I have already stated, I think that fly presentation is often more important than individual patterns, but there are times when fish will refuse all but the insects available at the moment. This is especially true at times when there is a major

hatch going on such as chironomid, mayfly or caddis hatches. Or, at times when there is an abundance of migrating insects available, such as the damselfly nymph. If you don't use a realistic imitation you might not do so well.

Most of the time I use patterns that generally imitate several insects, or, resemble nothing, but are just plain buggy-looking. I have been making a yearly excursion with friends to Washington state's Dry Falls Lake. It is tradition that I bring a new pattern to the lake each year. Usually the pattern I bring looks nothing like any aquatic insect available to the fish, yet it nearly always is a top producer on the trip. The reason being—it looks buggy, and I fish it in a seductive, realistic manner. The fact that I know the water real well doesn't hurt much either.

One of your biggest assets when fishing any water is that you do know it well. This simply comes from several fishing trips to that water, and an inquisitive attitude while there. Learn everything you can about the water. Where are the weed beds, drops, ledges, shallows, underwater springs, inlets, outlets, etc. Talk to those who appear

Desert lake nymph box.

to be doing well, and don't hesitate to ask questions. The more you know about a lake and its fish, the easier it will be to catch them.

When fishing from a float tube it is easy to get close to feeding fish. Since your profile is low on the water you spook fewer fish, and for this reason it is feasible to fish shallow, exposed areas where fish will sometimes be found feeding during low-light hours or on cloudy days. Seldom are long casts necessary and for this reason you have a great deal of line control. Short, precise casts are more desirable, especially when fishing to visible fish cruising, or to riseforms.

One point to keep in mind is that shady areas often hold fish at all times of the day. If you can find an area where a cliff, trees, or even shoreline vegetation like cattails provide shade on the water, work it well. Don't hesitate to cast your fly in tight against the

Casting to a rising trout in the Washington desert.

vegetation or that rock wall. Trout often hug these structures both for security and for the food sources they attract.

Besides working your fly in a natural manner, kicking erratically in your float tube, and getting to know the water you are fishing well, there is another technique you can use at times that will save the day, though few lake fly fishermen seem to do this on a regular basis. That technique is; using a full-sinking line, let your fly sink to the bottom. Make sure it is right on the bottom. Very slowly strip line in drawing your fly up. Raise it a few feet, and let it settle again. Repeat the process. I use this technique during the summer months when fish will often be found on the bottom. Takes are usually subtle, so you need to be on your toes.

Just remember, presentation and technique is everything. Trout feed, for the most part, everyday. Sometimes they can be difficult but, if they are present, you can catch them. It helps to think like a fish.

Fishing in
Dusty Lake,
eastern
Washington.

Seasons

Heavy hatch of chiefly chirono-mids around an arid Montana reservoir.

Each season offers something different when fishing any water. Desert and high arid lakes are no exception. Although spring and fall are probably the most pro-ductive months on the water, trout can be caught year-round, and indeed, many desert lakes around the west are open year-round. Sometimes tactics need to be changed a bit, but trout must eat, and that means that you can catch them.

Spring

Spring is probably the most productive time of year. The action starts just after ice-off in lakes that freeze over, and in late February/early March in lakes that don't. In other words, as soon as the water begins to warm a bit. Midges are the first insect that hatch in significant numbers, and the chironomid midge will be most important to the fly fisherman.

As the days grow warmer, weed growth begins to thrive in the shallows. The aquatic insects become active, and in most waters, trout fishing action is at its peak. Trout are on the cruise as their metabolism becomes more active due to warmer water temperatures. Fishing over weed beds will be the most productive this time of the year.

The shallows are much easier to fish during spring because the weed beds are just beginning to grow up. Because of weeds, many of the desert lakes have areas that are too shallow to fish at any other time than in spring. This is especially true if you are fishing from a doughnut-style float tube where your legs hang down.

Sitting in the shallows, you can watch cruising fish and cast a fly right into their path. Watching a big cruiser suck in your imitation is about as exciting as it gets. When fishing over the shallows, chirono-mids are hard to beat during spring months.

There will also be times when *Callibaetis* mayflies make a respectable appearance and, offer the cognizant angler some of the best dry fly action of the season. A Parachute Adams in the appropriate size will peg your fun meter for sure, if you are aware that fish are taking the mayflies. Since chironomids will more than likely still be coming off, many anglers fail to switch to flies that imitate *Callibaetis* and can't understand why the fish stopped hitting their chironomid fly.

Subsurface patterns like Zug-Bugs, and Gold Ribbed Hare's Ear Nymphs are also very effective when worked over and through the weeds. Trout are generally very willing to "chow down" on almost anything that looks like food and nearly any buggy looking fly pattern will often work if it is presented properly.

Wind can be a problem during spring in many of the desert lakes, especially those lakes within 100 miles east of the Cascade Mountain Range. This coastal range of mountains works as an effective moisture break for the desert areas to the east but the trade-off is the seemingly incessant winds of spring, sometimes howling for weeks at a time. Usually, if the weather forecast calls for rain on the coast, the desert areas of Washington and Oregon will be windy. Desert and arid lakes in other western states get their share of wind also, and spring seems to be the windiest time of year.

Spring is also the time of year when these lakes see the most pressure. Even though many of the lakes are open year-round, or open earlier than the general trout opener, there are a lot of anglers who wait until the general opener to try their luck. Come opening day there is a full-blown float tube hatch going on in many of the lakes, especially the most popular ones. I avoid fishing the first week of the season like the plague. After the first week of the opener things will gradually calm down and seldom are the waters too crowded to fish.

Summer

When spring gives way to the longer and warmer days of early summer, the chironomid hatches have slowed and, although they will continue until ice-up again, they occur heaviest during the morning and late evening hours. By this time in most of the lakes, damselfly and dragonfly nymphs will be on the move. An imitation of either will work quite nicely.

Fish are still very active in early summer, although many will be wise to the ways of the fly fisherman and your presentation will become most important.

As summer progresses the water will continue to warm and the activity will switch from the shallowest of water to water that is a little deeper and cooler, at least during the heat of the day. Sinking-tip lines will be used more than floating line and, activity during the day will slow.

Early morning and late evening will see most of the hatches, but night fishing is where it really happens during the heat of summer when fish are lethargic during daytime hours. Large leech patterns will account for most of the nighttime action.

If the lake you are fishing has underwater springs, and if you can locate those springs, you will most likely find a concentration of fish attracted by the cooler water. Trolling with a full-sinking line is probably the best way to locate underwater springs, or at least concentrations of fish.

Algae can be a problem on many of the more shallow lakes as the summer sun warms the water. If the lake is real shallow, decay of the algae can use too much of the oxygen from the lake and result in a summer kill. The biggest problem with algae for the fisherman in most waters is that it fouls your fly. It is imperative to constantly check your fly for gunk whenever it is present.

"Turnover" is a word that most lake fishermen have heard, but few really know what it means. It is really very simple. What basically happens is this. Many waters will stratify in temperature layers during summer. Since cold water is heavier than warm water, the warm water stays on top and the cold water is on the bottom of the lake. The area in between is known as the thermocline. When the warm water rapidly cools from rain, wind or cool nighttime temperatures, the now colder surface water begins to sink and comes in contact with the warmer water below. This forces the warmer bottom water to the top, and a mixing of the two takes place. You can often see bottom debris floating on the surface shortly after a turnover takes place.

A turnover can also take place in spring shortly after ice-off, as the colder surface water sinks to the bottom. Whenever a turnover takes place, one fact is certain; the fishing will be lousy for a few days!

Even on the best of days, fishing will be somewhat slow during the hot summer months in many of the desert lakes. For-

Desert wildflowers.

Small nymphs.

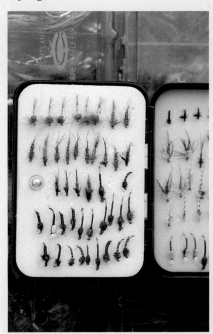

tunately, the hot summer nights don't last all that long, and give way to cool nights as fall approaches. Even though the days are still hot, the cool temperatures of night significantly lowers the water temperature, setting the stage for the fantastic fishing to be had during fall.

Fall

Fishing during fall is a close second to the productive times of spring. As water temperatures begin to cool in fall trout become more and more active. Although the hatches are nothing like those found during spring, trout will be gorging, getting ready for the lean months ahead.

By the time fall has arrived, many anglers have turned their attention to other things, like hunting, or they have just had enough fishing for the season. For whatever reasons, pressure on the lakes is much less during this time of year. Lakes that were crowded earlier during the season may now only host a handful of fishermen. Fall is my favorite time on the water.

Once again trout can be found cruising the shallows foraging for nearly any food item that gets in their path. It's time to store some fat for the cold winter months. Flies like Woolly Buggers in black or olive are hard to beat for numbers of fish. Fall is an especially good time to target big browns that have been chowing-down all season. Lakes that host these trout get plenty of my attention for sure!

Since water temperatures have cooled down considerably from summer trout will be less lethargic and will begin to feed throughout the day. The cold nights rid the water of algae growth, and as fall progresses the water will clear.

Late fall in the desert usually brings freezing nights and warm sunny days. The air is crisp and clear, the water clear and cold, and the trout are still gorging. Canadian honkers, headed for a more tolerable clime to spend the winter share the water with you. Fishing will be good until ice-up.

Winter

Open seasons vary considerably from state to state, but most states offer year-round fishing on at least some of their waters and some desert lakes and reservoirs are often included. Depending on the location, the lakes may or may not freeze over during winter. Those that don't can provide fishing the entire season. Those that do freeze over, and are open year-round, will usually only be out of service for a couple of months.

Cold weather float tubing isn't for everyone, of course, but to the devout trout addict it can be that needed "fix" to maintain sanity. Trout aren't real active when water temperatures are cold, so fishing must be slow and precise. Leeches worked ever so slowly across the bottom are your best hope for a cold water hook-up.

When tubing in extremely cold water you need to take many precautions to avoid becoming hypothermic. Pile bibs under your 5mm thick neoprene waders, and extra-thick socks, booties, gloves and a hat are a must. You simply can't have too many clothes along.

On warm winter days there can be a fairly significant hatch of midges that might provide some top-water fishing, but most likely you will be working the bottom with full-sinking lines and the leeches. At best, winter tubing the desert lakes will produce a few trout and keep you in contact with the water. It will also make you appreciate spring all that much more when it arrives!

Andy Anderson fishing Dry Falls on the last day of the open season.

Desert lake fly box full of nymphs.

WATCH FOR RATTLE SNAKES

Coiled rattlesnake, not an uncommon sight when fishing in deserts around the west.

Fly box filled with chironomids.

Float Tubes, Other Floating Craft, Accessories

The author fishing Lake Lenore from a Connic Boatman.

Float tubes and some of the newer personal boats on the market are by far the most efficient way to fish desert and high arid lakes. There are many reasons this is so. The most important, is that they allow you to meld into the trout's environment in silence. No creaky oars, or banging on the boat bottom to scare the fish. Your profile is low in the water, therefore, you are less apt to be seen, and will ultimately spook fewer fish. Tubes, and the personal boats, are very portable. They are easily packed, making it possible to hit that hidden lake, which would be impossible (or at least very difficult) to fish in any other way. And, since you are powered by swim fins, both hands are free to fish, allowing you to keep control of your rod and line at all times. No missed fish because you had to drop the oars and grab your rod, only to find that the fish already spit your fly!

There are many different types and styles of tubes and personal boats on the market. Prices vary, and usually reflect quality and features found on specific models. Many of the features are simply cosmetic and the decision on which to buy is simply which product appeals the most to your eye. My advice to people as far as float tubes are concerned, is to purchase a tube in the medium to top-end price range. If you buy a cheap tube, that's usually what you get—a cheap tube!

One feature that you should look for in a float tube or personal boat is a model with plenty of accessory pockets. You simply can't have too many pockets. Fly boxes, reel spools, rain jacket, camera, your lunch—you get the picture. They all take up room.

The doughnut-style float tube is the least expensive craft on the market. Most float tubes today are extremely well designed, with ample storage space for all your gear. Most have two large pockets in the back. One will hold a smaller inner-tube or air bladder for back-up flotation, and the other holds larger gear such as your jacket and lunch. Together the two back pockets make up the back-rest. Side pockets that connect to the back pockets are, in my opinion, the best design. When kicking into the wind they provide a barrier from the chop, and keep your arms from getting all wet. If there is a gap between the pockets the chop can splash through.

There are several useful accessories available for some float tube models. These include items such as; mesh creel, velcro rod holders, insulated drink holders, anchors and pack systems which allow you to easily make that trek to a distant lake. There are even depth/fish finders that strap right onto your tube or personal boat.

One of the biggest mistakes people make when new at float tubing is that they under-inflate their tube. When a tube is properly inflated it will have between two and three pounds of pressure in it. Float tube gauges are available at fly shops, and these are calibrated to only four pounds. Generally speaking though, if you inflate your tube just until all of the wrinkles are out of the fabric, it will be in that range. Personal boats are designed to operate on air pressures in that same range.

If you under-inflate your tube it will ride too low in the water, making it harder to operate, easier to get water over the back of your waders, and it is simply inefficient.

Some tubes are of an open front design. When doing seminars on float tubing I am often asked, "What's the advantage of an open front over the round ones?" Each design has advantages or disadvantages if you want to look at the differences like that, but I feel most of the differences are simply just a matter of personal choice. Many people like open front designs because you can just walk right up and sit down. They are definitely easier to get in and out of, which could be helpful in an emergency. You can go faster in an open front design, and there is no constricting tube above your legs. On the other hand, I like to lean my elbows on the front of a doughnut-style tube while I fish on, and you certainly can't do that with an open front model.

In my fishing I use both types of tubes and I can't really say which style I like best—I like them both. Most of the tubes on the market are well designed fishing crafts, and all have their own unique features. Some are cosmetic, many are design differences that will fit individual body shapes or intended uses better. For example; the open-front tubes use PVC or other lightweight bladders instead of the conventional inner-tube, cutting the weight drastically, they also have the ability to be blown up by mouth and therefore are more practical for backpacking. It's best to take into consideration everything you intend to do with a tube and try different tube designs before you buy if you have the opportunity. Friends, other fishermen on the water, or sports shows are possibilities for trying out different crafts.

Every season there are more and more personal fishing crafts available on the market. They range from one-man rafts with no floor to mini pontoon boats. Most are for use in lakes and ponds, but some of the mini-boats have oar systems making moderate river travel possible.

Again, when doing tubing seminars at sports shows I am often asked what advantage the new boats have over float tubes. And again, I explain the differences. In general, little personal boats do almost everything a float tube will, and then some. They ride higher, are easy to get in and out of, kick considerably faster, but they also cost a little more. Some people swear by these little fishing machines. I'm one, and I have several. But I also have several float tubes, both doughnut-style and open end. I like them all, and use them all. It really boils down to personal choice, with factors such as how often you

intend to fish, the types of water you fish, how big your wallet is, etc., to be considered.

Since you are sitting in the water while float tubing, and higher, yet subject to splash in personal boats, you must wear chest-high waders to stay dry. The stocking foot type are most practical. Unless you are properly insulated from the water's chill, tubing can be a miserable affair, if not downright life-threatening. One always needs to be cognizant of the fact that hypothermia is a possibility in this sport. To avoid misery or death (neither of which I think we all agree are desirable) there is one simple solution— neoprene. Unless it is mid-summer and the water is very warm, you will get cold wearing any other type of stocking foot wader. Neoprene will insulate you from even the coldest water if you wear appropriate clothes underneath, such as wicking underwear, pile bibs, or any of the other synthetic cold weather clothes designed for outdoor activities.

When neoprene waders spring a leak (all waders will eventually leak) they are easily fixed with Aquaseal or Simmseal. Waders usually begin to leak around the crotch area or other high stress seam areas like the knees. The problem is, you can seldom visualize the point of the

Ron Meek with a rainbow caught at Buckhorn Ranch, a pay fishery in central Oregon.

actual leak because the seams are usually taped. So, you have the leaky roof syndrome—water comes in one place and shows up at another. What you end up doing in this case is smearing one of the aforementioned products over the entire area and it usually fixes the problem.

Even when you spring a leak in your neoprene waders, you seldom have to stop fishing because of it. In fact, most of the time you don't realize you have a leak until you get out of the water for the day, pull your waders off, and notice that you are wet. The leak is usually small, and due to the incredible insulating effects of neoprene, the moisture is quickly warmed to body temperature.

Over the feet of your waders you should wear booties of some sort. The best ones are made of neoprene and are designed specifically for this purpose. Booties provide extra insulation from the cold, have a hard sole for walking around parking lots or walking back to you car after being blown to the other end of the lake, etc. Booties will also save wear and tear on the ankle area of your waders from your fin straps.

There are several types of fins available, and all will work for float tubing. Several things need to be considered when buying fins. Force Fins are probably the easiest fins I have ever used for general float tubing. They are lightweight, the front is turned up making it possible to walk on flat ground without stumbling, and you can kick them all day long—effortlessly. Diving-type graphite fins will let you push more water, and are great for covering large areas, or tubing in the wind. On the downside, they take a bit of effort to power, and if your legs are not in shape, after a day of tubing you will definitely know you did something. There are fins available that fit over wading shoes which are great for those who have boot-foot waders, and there are now flat, lightweight fins, great for backpacking.

The main thing in buying fins is to make sure they fit your feet right. At least half the people I fish with complain that their feet are cold or that they get cramps after being in the water awhile. This is almost always caused by fins that don't fit their feet properly. What usually happens is that they buy waders, then fins, and later on decide that booties would be nice. By the time all the components are put together, the fins cramp their feet. If your feet are cramped on dry ground, you can rest assured that your toes will get cold and your feet will cramp even worse when you get into the water. My advice is to buy your fins on the large side in anticipation of wearing booties—if you don't already own some. And, if you are in the market for new fins, take your waders and booties along when heading off to purchase them. Put all your gear on, including the socks you intend to wear, and try several fins on. When properly fit, you should be able to move your toes around just like your were wearing a pair of comfortable shoes.

Most tubers don't wear fishing vests because the bottom pockets get wet, even on most of the shorty vests. Chest tackle packs are nice, but with the large pocket designs available on most tubes and personal boats you have plenty of room for all your gear without wearing a vest.

It doesn't take long to get the hang of float tubing or operating one of the personal boats. Propelling with swim fins is awkward for some at first, but it only takes a short period of time before navigation becomes second-nature. If your fins fit right and don't make your feet cramp up, you can float tube for hours on end—effortlessly. After awhile you completely forget about the mechanics of kicking and find yourself just moving around in

Cindy Probasco fishing Lake Lenore in a Wood River Gliderider float tube.

Pinky
Freeman with
a nice desert
rainbow.

the water to rises, or moving to different areas, oblivious to everything but the moment at hand.

You can effectively tube even under windy conditions. Where a small boat would be blown around and impossible to control, a tube may allow you to fish the same water without a problem. A boat riding on the surface catches a lot of wind and is tossed around. Since a tube is smaller, and your profile is low in the water, you catch a lot less wind. And, in a small boat you need to keep your hands on the oars or stay anchored. In a tube your oars are on your feet, keeping your hands free for fishing. It only makes sense that you will catch more fish if you keep your hands on your rod.

Since your center of gravity in a tube is below the waterline, they are a very stable craft. As with any water-craft, common sense goes a long way, and there are some definite things to consider to make this sport as safe as possible. You should always have a backup flotation device. A car inner-tube or other type of air bladder should always be inflated in the compartment provided on most modern tubes. I wouldn't use a tube if it didn't have a spare flotation chamber in the event that something happened to my main air compartment. In addition, in my tube I carry a folded up life vest in the other back compartment. When I am in the water I am reasonably sure no ill will come to me because I have the main chamber, back-up chamber, life vest and am wearing highly buoyant neoprene waders.

It is unlikely that your tube will suddenly deflate because at the low pressures which they are filled it would take a long time to lose enough air from a hook puncture (the most common puncture) to cause a problem. It's not like you are going to sink a hook into your tube and blow all around the lake deflating, like you might expect in a cartoon. It won't happen. Besides, the tight woven nylon covering of most float tubes is highly resistant to hook penetration in the first place. In my 20 years of tubing I have never punctured my tube with a hook or any other object.

You should check your inner-tube at least twice a year though, just to make sure it is not cracked or damaged in any way. After all, they are made of rubber, and rubber will rot. If you store your tube dry, out of direct sunlight and in a place where other objects can't be thrown on top of it, it will last a long time.

I have heard of sudden deflations, but the causes I'm not sure of. I know of at least one that was due to a rotten inner-tube. I did hear of a sudden deflation by a guy who decided to cut a salami for his lunch one day, using his tube for a cutting board. When he told me the tale, he said that he felt tubes should be made stronger. I felt that he shouldn't even be float tubing. Like I said, common sense goes a long way.

In the event of a problem it would be nice to have a prompt rescue, and for that reason alone it's a good idea to float with another person, or around other tubers on a lake.

As far as stability goes, like I mentioned, when you are properly fit in a float tube your center of gravity will be just below the waterline. That's not saying that you can't flip over, but you would have to do something incredibly stupid to do so, or be too big for the tube you are in. In my 20 years of float tubing I have witnessed two tubers flip their tubes. Both were due to gross human error. The first was a guy who unthinkingly scooted up on the backrest while trying to adjust his seat strap. It doesn't take a rocket scientist to figure that one out—

Ticks are a constant problem when fishing desert lakes.

Ken Bamford with a rainbow from a desert lake.

he went over. The other time I saw a tube flip was during a windstorm. An incredible windstorm, that kept everyone off the water except this one person. There were five-foot standing waves on the water. I watched as his tube crested a wave, caught a wind gust, and flew ten feet through the air before touching down. When it did, the tube was upside down. The tuber escaped unharmed, although understandably shaken. Again, common sense would have prevented this.

I'm sure that there are other incidents where people have had serious problems while float tubing. I have heard several stories, everything from lightning striking a tube to cottonmouth snake, alligator and shark attacks. Use your noodle, and you shouldn't get into a fix you can't get out of.

Night Fishing

Night fishing sounds a bit loony to many people who have never tried it. I can't count the number of times that I have been lakeside getting gear ready for a night's fishing, only to be questioned and chortled at by fellow anglers who surely thought I was stark-raving mad. What on earth would possess a man of sound mind to get into a float tube and paddle out into a lake in total darkness? Well, that's an easy one for me to answer because I do it all the time. Trout! Big trout...It's a simple question to answer!

It's no secret that large trout feed at night. This is especially true of big, weary brown trout. After-hours angling can reveal some fascinating results for those willing to brave the darkness. To put it quite simply; the angler who fishes at night is going to catch larger, and often

more, fish than those who just fish during daylight hours.

Sure, there are some disadvantages to night fishing, and night fishing isn't for everyone. Nothing is. But for those of stout mind, and in water where it is allowed, night fishing is truly a way to tie into some very large fish, larger than those found in the same water during the day.

Desert trout are especially good targets for the night fisherman, and the hot summer months are best. The trout's metabolism is up when the water temperatures are warm and they must eat a lot of food. During the heat of day the fish lay low and are lethargic. When water temperatures drop a little during the darkness of night the water comes alive—trout will be feeding on anything that moves.

There are many points to consider before you head out on a night fishing excursion. Nothing seems as easy as it does during the light of day. It's harder to tie on flies, your leader seems to tangle more often—just about everything you do appears to be harder—because you can't see. Your techniques and skills need to be finely tuned so that mistakes are at a minimum. Murphy's Law seems to take over at night, and "everything that can go wrong, will." If you tend to get frustrated easily—forget it. Night fishing might not be for you.

Fishing the evening hatch in a western reservoir.

You must consider the danger aspect of night fishing. Whether you are wading from shore, or fishing from a tube or boat, you must know the water you are fishing. Don't get yourself into a hazardous situation. Keep all the obstacles you may encounter in mind. It's easy to get turned around in the dark. Don't fish alone, and use your noodle. Common sense is imperative.

Shallow lakes that taper out gradually from shore are easy to fish by just wading out a ways. Long casts are not necessary as trout feed in close to the shore at night, much less fearful of predators than during the daylight. Many times fish can be hooked within inches of the shore. I don't really like walking the shoreline at night in desert settings because rattlesnakes often materialize near the water's edge when the sun goes down. I feel much better in a float tube.

For night fishing I always use heavier gear than I would on the same water during daylight hours. Most often I use a 6-weight fast action graphite rod equipped with a full-floating line. My leaders are never longer than three feet in length, and are usually nothing more than a twelve inch, heavy butt, to which is attached a two foot section of 0X tippet material.

Trout zero in on food items at night, largely by the vibration they make in the water. For this reason, use big patterns during the night. My absolute favorite pattern at night (I only use two patterns) is a monstrous leech I simply call my Night Leech. This fly seems to outproduce all other flies—hands down!

I like fishing this leech on a floating line, casting to shore, or over shallow weed beds. Long casts are not necessary, and only increase the chances for error. Short, controlled casts are best, with slow strips of the line. You can expect some pretty violent takes, as these night feeders are not usually bashful.

The only other fly I use for night fishing is a mouse pattern. I use this fly when the lake I am fishing has steep banks or rocky shorelines where mice sometimes fall in the water and become trout food. Big trout food!

When fishing a mouse pattern I use a sink-tip line and, again, a short leader. I will sit out about twenty feet from the shore and cast my mouse to within inches of the bank. I let it land with a "plop." If a big trout doesn't nail it immediately, I

swim it around erratically. If this gets no results and the water is deep enough I let the sink-tip settle a bit then give a sharp tug on the

line which will draw the mouse under, creating a noise as if it just fell in. No self respecting trout can refuse this. If there is a feeding trout nearby it will come to investigate, and most often will take the mouse on its float back to the surface. If this still doesn't produce a fish—move, or try again. Sooner or later the water will explode!

I have found moonless nights, nights that are pitch black, offer the best fishing. I have sat under the moonlight making cast after hopeless cast into water that I knew held fish, only to have a cloud pass in front of the moon, lessening the intensity of light and, bingo! The trout began to hit, only to stop as soon as the moon's full force hits the water again. If you are forced to fish on nights with a full moon, you are better off using a full-sinking line and going down deep where the light intensity is not nearly as great.

Night fishing requires you to pack a few more items of gear. A flex light will help when tying on flies. A high-powered, waterproof flashlight will often come in handy when trying to find your way off the water. Temperatures in the desert can cool rapidly at night, so an extra jacket might be in order also.

If you tend to doze off easily, it might be wise to rig a runaway strap from your rod to your vest or tube to avoid losing an expensive rod and reel. I fall asleep all the time while fishing at night. It's not a problem though, actually it's kind of fun.

Desert friends.

Steve Probasco with a night-caught brown.

Western Pay Lakes

Steve Probasco with a Minnie Lake, B.C. rainbow.

Every trout fisher has that dream of catching a truly big fish—a monster trout, like those found hanging on the walls of fishing lodges. Those fish from yester-year; the kind that old-timers talk about,

but for the most part are now gone from public waters. With increasing fishing pressure on the water, and put-and-take mentalities and regulations that are so prevalent, that's to be expected—the destiny of poorly managed public water. Many of the "dream lakes" of yesteryear now only yield small, hatchery fish whose fate is bleak, to say the least.

Across the west there are an increasing number of fisheries adopting limited, and no-kill, regulations to help produce quality water, and it's working in most cases, with more and larger fish available to the angler. But it often takes more time and money than the regulating agencies can come up with to aggressively provide the ideal set of conditions conducive to optimal fish habitat and growth on a widespread basis. Instead, only a few public waters get the attention they really need. And besides, they still have the kill-a-limit crowd to contend with, and they buy a heck of a lot of fishing licenses.

Over the past several years there have been several pay-to-fish lakes entering the scene around the west. A few adventuresome folk have realized the desire (and willingness to pay) of many fly fishermen to catch large trout, and thus catered to this desire by developing exceptional trout fisheries in select lakes on privately owned land. This is not a cheap, or easy, endeavor. Trout don't grow to enormous proportions by accident, there are many factors involved. In many cases the attempts to produce monster trout have failed—for a variety of reasons. In some cases, however, the efforts produced in a big way, with trout averaging much larger than all but a few that are taken out of public water.

There are some who believe it a sin to pay for the opportunity to fish any water. One needs to keep things in perspective though. There is a tremendous expense in developing and maintaining such a fishery, and when the management and politics of our public fisheries has failed (for various reasons) to produce the quality of trouting that so many of us desire, who is to condemn those who take it upon themselves to produce such a fishery? More and more anglers are realizing the value of the new pay-to-play resource and are willing to pay the price. In fact, many of the pay waters are booked a whole season in advance.

I have fished several of the pay lakes around the west. There are many that I

haven't yet fished, and currently, several in the making. Some of the first pay lakes I fished are now the oldest in operation— testimony that this type of fishery is here to stay.

Grindstone Lake, in central Oregon was the first pay lake I ever fished. Actually, the first time I ever fished it the pay-to-play idea was still in the making. I traveled to this "secret lake" with friends Randall Kaufmann and Brian O'Keefe to sample the fishing for monster trout that Brian had told me about. What we found were rainbows in the five to nine pound range. At the time, those were the largest rainbows I had ever caught. As you can expect, the images of those trout are forever fixed in my mind.

Roughly around that same time, George Cook began an operation in central Washington in an area now known as Ranch Lakes. Fishing is similar to that found in Grindstone Lakes, with trophy sized trout the rule. The reason? Careful management, with catch-and-release of all trout.

While traveling the western states, I have found that pay-to-play lakes are pretty much consistent in the quality of fishing found. I believe that quality pay lakes are the wave of the future, and endeavors by those who make it all happen deserve a hand. They are making it possible for more people to enjoy the thrill of trophy

fishing without the exorbitance of traveling to remote parts of the world. I guess what it really boils down to is this; how much would you pay to catch 5 to 10 pound rainbows all day long?

Since there are new pay lakes

Ron Meek with a Grindstone Lake rainbow.

popping up all the time, to list the ones I know of at this time would be incomplete to those who might read this book in a couple of years. The best way to find out what pay lakes are available in any given part of the west would be to call a local fly shop in that area.

Large, high arid lake rainbow.

Useful Flies

Desert rainbow.

To list all of the flies that are useful when fishing desert and high arid lakes would fill an entire book. And everyone who fishes these lakes has their own favorites. There are some common imitations, standard ties that are time proven that everyone has, such as Gold Ribbed Hare's Ear Nymphs, Woolly Buggers, etc.

Most lake fishermen eventually design their own patterns though, to imitate the aquatic insects found in the particular waters they fish.

In this chapter I share with you the flies I use most often when fishing lakes. There's nothing too earth shattering here, basic designs that do a good job of imitating the aquatic insects found in most lakes. My goal when tying flies is not to see how fancy or exactly I can imitate any given insect, but rather to tie workable and easily tied patterns, flies that catch fish and can be turned out in a minute or two. Almost every pattern featured here falls under these guidelines.

As I mentioned before in this book, I feel that presentation is much more important than specific fly design. I think that a general imitation fished properly will put more bend in your rod than a precise pattern fished sloppy.

As time goes on, more and more synthetic materials are hitting the fly tying market. Some of these materials are remarkable, and only add to the ease and efficiency of tying some patterns. I am not stuck on the use of either natural or synthetics, and I often mix the two.

Many of the flies featured here are spinoffs of standards, or innovative patterns that I came across at one time or another. I experiment a lot when tying, and encourage you to do the same. A different twist on materials or design can sometimes culminate in a pattern that's a hit.

Use this section as a guide for your tying. These are the flies I use, but as I said, this is by no means a comprehensive list of what will work for desert trout.

Red Leech

Hook: Daiichi 2220, size no. 6 to no. 8
Thread: Red
Tail: Red marabou
Body: Red leech yarn

Tying Steps

Step 1: Tie in one red marabou feather. Make sure ends are even.

Step 2: Tie in a piece of red leech yarn and wind forward. Finish head and cement.

This is a fly that is a bit off-the-wall in that it doesn't really look like anything trout actually encounter. I have seen times though when this pattern has saved our bacon, so to speak. I think that some-

times fish are on the lookout for something a bit different. If so, this fly certainly fills that bill.

Fish this pattern on the bottom just as you would any leech pattern, with a slow retrieve. When things are a little slow, this bright red pattern just might save the day.

Snail

Hook: Daiichi 1150, size no. 12 to no. 16
Thread: Olive
Underbody: Lead wire
Body: Peacock herl
Ribbing: Copper wire
Hackle: Brown neck hackle, fore and aft

Tying Steps

Step 1: Wind the center portion of the hook with lead wire.
Step 2: Tie in a brown neck hackle at the butt of the fly and wind one or two turns.
Step 3: Secure three or four strands of peacock herl at the front of the fly. Wind them back over the lead wire and then forward to the front of the fly.
Step 4: Tie in a piece of copper wire in front of the body and wind over the herl, then forward crossing over the strands you wound back.
Step 5: Tie in another hackle in front of the body, wind one or two turns, finish the head and cement.

I first heard of using snail patterns while talking with Gary Borger at a FFF Conclave in West Yellowstone, Montana. We were talking about desert lakes and he asked me if I had ever used snail flies while fishing in Washington state. At the time I had never even considered it.

This snail design is the one Gary told me about (or at least the way I remember him describing it) during our conversation. It wasn't until several months later that I tried the fly. Things were a bit slow on one of my favorite lakes. Looking through a fly box I came across a few of the snails that I, as of then still viewed with skepticism, and decided to give one a try.

The rest is history. I nailed the trout, while nearly everyone else continued to have a slow day. Needless to say, I was sold on snail flies when fishing desert lakes. I have used several snail designs since, but feel that this one works best. The hackle adds a bit of movement to catch the fish's eye, and the herl and copper combo give the color appearance of a natural snail.

Water Boatman

Hook: Daiichi 1270, size no. 10 or no. 12
Thread: Tan
Body: Tan dubbing (with sparkle)
Shellback/Wings: Turkey quill
Legs: Turkey quill

Tying Steps

Step 1: Secure a section of turkey quill to the hook at the butt of the fly.
Step 2: Dub a thick body of your favorite dubbing material. I prefer a dubbing with a bit of sparkle to it, which helps emulate the air bubble that the water boatman descends with. Wind the body 2/3 the way up the hook shank.
Step 3: Isolate a couple of fibers of turkey quill and tie in above the body dubbed on thus far.
Step 4: Continue dubbing on the body to the head of the fly.
Step 5: Pull the turkey quill over the body and tie down at the head to form the shellback/wings.
Step 6: Finish head and cement the entire shellback with Daves's Fleximent or similar product to complete the Water Boatman.

The Water Boatman is a pattern that is useful in most lakes at certain times. Trout seem to either attack them with enthusiasm or completely ignore them. Spring and fall seem to be the most productive times for fishing them.

Water Boatman collect an air bubble from the surface, then descend with the bubble trapped beneath their body. They swim around erratically using their oarlike legs (thus their name) and imitations should be fished in a like manner.

This pattern can be effectively fished from top to bottom using full-floating, sinking-tip or full-sinking lines, depending on where the trout are taking insects at the moment. The key to this pattern's success, as I mentioned, is fishing it with an erratic retrieve.

Black Bead Chain Nymph

Hook: Daiichi 1710, size no. 10 to no. 14
Thread: Black
Tail: Grizzly hackle fibers
Abdomen: Black dubbing
Ribbing: Silver wire
Thorax: Silver wire

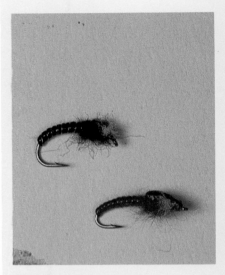

Chironomid pupae patterns.

Whitlock Mouse.

Crayfish patterns.

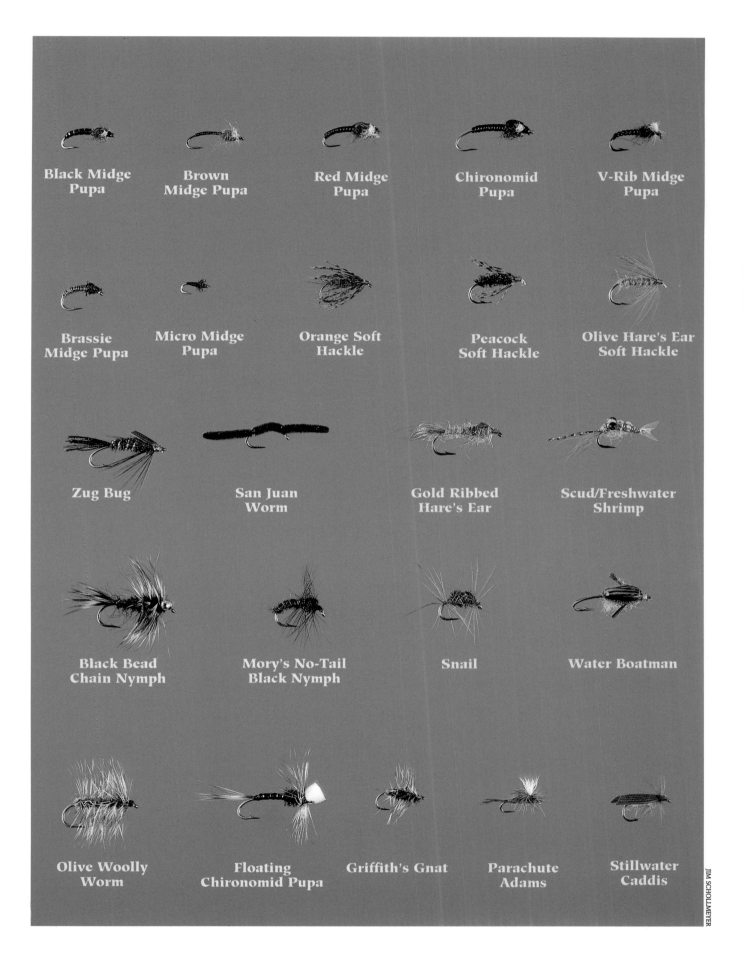

Black Midge
Pupa

Brown
Midge Pupa

Red Midge
Pupa

Chironomid
Pupa

V-Rib Midge
Pupa

Brassie
Midge Pupa

Micro Midge
Pupa

Orange Soft
Hackle

Peacock
Soft Hackle

Olive Hare's Ear
Soft Hackle

Zug Bug

San Juan
Worm

Gold Ribbed
Hare's Ear

Scud/Freshwater
Shrimp

Black Bead
Chain Nymph

Mory's No-Tail
Black Nymph

Snail

Water Boatman

Olive Woolly
Worm

Floating
Chironomid Pupa

Griffith's Gnat

Parachute
Adams

Stillwater
Caddis

JIM SCHOLLMEYER

Hackle: Grizzly
Eyes: Silver bead chain

Tying Steps

Step 1: Tie in a small bunch of grizzly hackle fibers for the tail.

Step 2: Secure a piece of silver wire to the hook, dub on the abdomen, and wind the wire forward as a rib.

Step 3: Cut a section of bead chain and tie in at the head using a figure-eight motion of the tying thread.

Step 4: Tie in a grizzly neck hackle by the tip.

Step 5: Dub on a thorax that is twice as thick as the abdomen and wind the hackle forward.

Step 6: Finish head and cement to complete the Black Bead Chain Nymph.

This fly doesn't closely imitate any particular insect, but looks incredibly buggy, and is one of my very favorite search patterns when the fishing is slow. The bead chain eyes make the fly swim point up, making it less likely to snag as it swims through the weeds.

The success I experience with this fly only strengthens my feeling that many times it doesn't matter so much the fly you use, but the manner in which it is fished. When this fly is worked seductively through weed beds, or slowly over the bottom, it is one of the most productive flies in my desert box.

Black Woolly Bugger

Hook: Daiichi 2220, size no. 6 to no. 14
Thread: Black
Tail: Black marabou
Body: Black leech yarn
Hackle: Black saddle hackle

Tying Steps

Step 1: Tie in a stem of marabou, making sure that the fibers form an even tail.

Step 2: Secure a piece of black leech yarn and a black saddle hackle by the tip to the hook shank, at the butt of the fly.

Step 3: Wind the yarn forward and secure at the head. Now wind the hackle forward and secure at the head.

Step 4: Finish the head and cement to complete the Black Woolly Bugger.

The Black Woolly Bugger probably accounts for more fish from stillwaters than any other fly. Fish are most likely taking it for a leech, which are found in most waters. The Woolly Bugger has taken its share of fish for me, and is still one of my first choices when fishing water that I know holds large trout.

The most effective way to fish this fly is slowly, and on the bottom. Many fishermen like to troll the Bugger behind a tube or boat, and this works well also. The key, however, is to fish it slowly.

The Woolly Bugger can be tied in a variety of colors, and using a variety of materials. I most often use the standard, Black Woolly Bugger, but Buggers in olive, brown, tan, purple and a host of other colors are sometimes effective.

Nearly any body material available can be used for tying this fly also. Chenille, dubbing, yarn, etc. can be used. Krystal Flash or other flashy materials tied in the tail and along the body of this fly are also used. This is a pattern with which you can be very creative.

Crystal Carey

Hook: TMC 7989, size no. 10 or no. 12
Body: Crystal Chenille—red, green, brown, etc.
Hackle: Pheasant rump feather

Tying Steps

Step 1: Tie in a piece of Crystal Chenille and wind forward to form the body.

Step 2: Secure a pheasant rump feather by the tip and wind two or three turns.

Step 3: Finish head and cement to complete the Crystal Carey.

The Carey Special has been a favorite lake pattern in stillwaters since people began fishing stillwaters. Many people have forgotten about this fly, as it gets little attention in fishing magazines, tying books, etc. Still, the Carey Special is a productive fly when fishing any water for trout.

Most of the Carey Specials I tie these days are tied using Crystal Chenille for the body material. This material has bulk, flash and movement, which I think adds to the effectiveness of the fly. Olive and red are the two colors I use most for my Crystal Careys.

Although this fly doesn't closely resemble any particular aquatic insect, when tied in the appropriate sizes it does a fair job of emulating dragonfly nymphs, emerging caddis and a few other critters found in stillwaters.

Woolly Worm

Hook: Daiichi 1720, size no. 6 to no. 16

Thread: Maroon
Body: Olive Chenille
Hackle: Grizzly

Tying Steps

Step 1: Tie in a piece of olive chenille (sized to hook) and a grizzly neck hackle by the tip.

Step 2: Wind the chenille and then the hackle forward, securing both at the head.

Step 3: Finish head and cement to complete the Woolly Worm.

The Woolly Worm is a fly that has been around forever. It is the first pattern that most tiers perfect. It is a simple fly that is still one of the standards for trout. Too bad many lake fishermen have forgotten about it.

I most often tie my Woolly Worms in small sizes, and in olive, yellow, black or brown. The Woolly Worm featured here, size no. 12, olive with maroon head, is my usual choice when fishing desert lakes. This fly resembles scuds, damsel nymphs, small leeches, etc. It is a pattern that certainly reserves a large corner of my desert fly box.

The Woolly Worm can be fished at any depth using a variety of lines, depending on the insect you intend to imitate. Or, the Woolly Worm can be trolled at various depths, and is highly effective when fished in this manner.

Bug Eye Bugger

Hook: Daiichi 2220, size no. 6 to no. 14
Thread: Black
Tail: Black marabou
Body: Olive Chenille
Hackle: Black
Eyes: Yellow no-toxic eyes

Tying Steps

Step 1: Tie in a marabou tail just as with the standard Woolly Bugger.

Step 2: Wind on a body of olive chenille and palmer a black saddle hackle over the body.

Step 3: Tie on the eyes using a figure-eight motion of the thread.

Step 4: Finish head and cement to complete the Bug Eye Bugger.

When fishing deeper water, Buggers tied with lead eyes make the task a lot easier. Plus, the weighted eyes give the fly a jigging action when retrieved.

Besides the olive body, black and purple are good colors also. I use this fly

Damselfly Nymph

Adult Damsel

Dragonfly Nymph

Green Crystal Carey

Red Crystal Carey

Bug Eye Bugger

Night Leech

Red Leech

Black Woolly Bugger

Mouse

Crayfish

often when fishing lakes that I know contain big trout, and this fly has accounted for its share of truly large fish for me.

Griffith's Gnat

Hook: TMC 101, size no. 16
Thread: Olive
Body: Peacock herl
Hackle: Grizzly

Tying Steps

Step 1: Tie in a single strand of peacock herl and a grizzly neck hackle by the tip.
Step 2: Wind the herl and then the hackle forward.
Step 3: Finish head and cement to complete the Griffith's Gnat.

The Griffith's Gnat is great when trout are taking adult or stillborn midges on the surface. Cast it out into an area where fish are actively feeding. Keep a keen eye, and a tight line. If your leader dips under, quickly but gently raise your rod tip. Sometimes it is more effective to clip the hackle off the top and bottom of the fly. This will let it ride lower in the surface film, and does a better job of imitating the stillborn midge.

Brassie Midge Pupa

Hook: TMC 2457, size no. 14 or no. 16
Thread: Black
Body: Fine copper wire
Head: Black ostrich herl

Tying Steps

Step 1: Secure a piece of copper wire to the hook shank and wind forward.
Step 2: Tie in a piece of ostrich herl and wind two or three turns.
Step 3: Finish head and cement to complete the Brassie Midge Pupa.

This fly is a good choice when trout are taking midge pupas from top to bottom. When my standard chironomid patterns fail to produce, and fishing is slow with other patterns, I often use this fly.

My usual way to fish the Brassie Midge Pupa is to cast out and let the fly sink to the bottom. I then slowly strip line up with a slight jigging action, eventually working the fly to the surface. If I get concentrations of strikes in any one depth, I focus my efforts there, of course.

Gold Ribbed Hare's Ear Nymph

Hook: Daiichi 1710, size no. 10 to no. 18

Thread: Tan
Tail: Guard hairs from English hare's mask
Abdomen: Dubbed fur from hare's mask, without guard hairs
Ribbing: Gold wire
Thorax: Dubbed fur from hare's mask with guard hairs mixed in
Wingcase: Turkey quill

Tying Steps

Step 1: Tie on a short tail of guard hairs.
Step 2: Secure a piece of gold wire to the hook, dub a thin abdomen 2/3 the way up the hook shank and then rib with the wire.
Step 3: Tie in a piece of turkey quill for the wingcase.
Step 4: Dub on a thicker thorax of the fur from the hare's mask with guard hairs mixed in.
Step 5: Pull the turkey quill over the thorax and secure, forming the wingcase.
Step 6: Pick thorax fur with a bodkin or dubbing teaser to make guard hairs stand out, finish head and cement to complete the Gold Ribbed Hare's Ear Nymph.

If I had to fish the desert and high arid lakes with just one fly, the Gold Ribbed Hare's Ear Nymph would be that fly. This pattern has accounted for more fish for me than any other—hands down!

When tied in different sizes this fly resembles many different aquatic insects. Besides the natural hare's mask color, this fly can also be tied in olive or black, using hare's masks that have been dyed.

Fished at any level, the Gold Ribbed Hare's Ear Nymph, in a variety of sizes and colors should be included in the fly boxes of everyone who fishes desert and high arid lakes.

Parachute Adams

Hook: TMC 100, size no. 12 to no. 20
Thread: Gray
Tail: Mixed brown and grizzly hackle fibers
Body: Gray dubbing
Wing: White poly yarn
Hackle: One brown and one grizzly hackle

Tying Steps

Step 1: Mix a few brown and a few grizzly hackle fibers together and tie in for a tail.

Step 2: Tie in a wing of poly yarn, parachute style.
Step 3: Dub on the body using your favorite dubbing material, tapering slightly larger towards the head. Stop winding on the dubbing just short of the wing.
Step 4: Tie in one brown and one grizzly hackle and wind two or three turns around the post, parachute style.
Step 5: Add more dubbing to your thread and carefully wind forward to the head.
Step 6: Finish head and cement to complete the Parachute Adams.

Callibaetis mayflies are the most common mayfly found in desert and high arid lakes. When hatches of this fairly large mayfly are present trout feed voraciously on them. Often, the hatch will happen along with chironomids, and anglers fail to switch to an adult mayfly pattern even though the trout already have.

The Parachute Adams does a good job of imitating the *Callibaetis*. The hatch will often be short lived, so the fisherman cognizant of its happening, and with a few Parachute Adams in his or her box, will be in for some hot action.

Hare's Ear Soft Hackle

Hook: Mustad 94834 (gold hook) or standard nymph hook, size no. 12 to no. 16
Thread: Brown
Body: Natural hare's ear dubbing
Rib: Gold wire
Hackle: Brown hen hackle

Tying Steps

Step 1: Secure a piece of gold wire to the hook, dub on a ragged body of hare's ear dubbing and then wind wire forward to form the rib.
Step 2: Tie in a dark brown hen hackle and wind two or three turns.
Step 3: Finish head and cement to complete the Hare's Ear Soft Hackle.

Soft hackled patterns work well nearly everywhere as they closely resemble many emerging insects. They can be tied in different sizes and colors to emulate specific insects, and when worked through the water offer seductive, trout catching movement.

I like to tie my soft hackles on gold hooks, which I feel adds to the effectiveness of the fly. However, if gold hooks aren't available, any standard nymph hook will work fine.

San Juan Worm

Hook: Daiichi 1150, size no. 12 to no. 15
Thread: Red
Body: Red Ultra Chenille

Tying Steps

Step 1: Secure a one-inch piece of Ultra Chenille to the hook by wrapping a few tight turns at the butt, middle and at the head of the fly as shown. The entire hook shank should be wrapped with thread under the chenille.

Step 2: Taper the ends of the chenille with a match, or some other heat source by bringing the heat close— just until the ends shrivel.

Step 3: Finish head and cement to complete the San Juan Worm.

The San Juan Worm imitates the red midge larva that burrows in the bottom muck of a lake where oxygen levels are low. Commonly known as bloodworms, the red coloration is due to the hemoglobin in their blood.

A San Juan Worm slowly danced over the bottom using whatever line required to get it there can be deadly.

Zug Bug

Hook: Daiichi 1270, size no. 10 to no. 16
Thread: Olive
Tail: Peacock herl
Body: Peacock herl
Ribbing: Silver Mylar
Wingcase: Turkey quill
Hackle: Furnace

Tying Steps

Step 1: Tie in a few tapered ends of peacock herl to form a short tail.

Step 2: Wind on a body of peacock herl, tapered slightly larger towards the head. Wind on the ribbing.

Step 3: Tie in a piece of turkey quill and clip short for a wingcase.

Step 4: Tie on a sparse beard of furnace hackle.

Step 5: Finish the head and cement to complete the Zug Bug.

The Zug Bug is another of those patterns that should be in every lake fisher's fly box. Like the Gold Ribbed Hare's Ear Nymph, the Zug Bug emulates several aquatic insects when tied in a variety of sizes.

Fish the Zug Bug through the weeds, along the shoreline or along the bottom. Use it during the damselfly emergence, mayfly hatches, or when there are no hatches. This pattern can be effective when fished in just about any manner or season.

Mory's No-Tail Black Nymph

Hook: Daiichi 1150, size no. 10 to no. 14
Thread: Black
Abdomen: Black dubbing
Ribbing: Copper wire
Thorax: Black dubbing
Hackle: Black neck hackle

Tying Steps

Step 1: Wind on an abdomen of black dubbing and rib with copper wire.

Step 2: Tie in a black neck hackle by the tip and then dub on a thorax twice as thick as the abdomen.

Step 3: Palmer the hackle forward to the head and secure.

Step 4: Finish head and cement to complete Mory's No-Tail Black Nymph.

I first fished this fly while on a fishing trip down in Chili. The guide (Mory) suggested giving the fly a try. Of course it worked, and when I returned home I experimented with this pattern on all types of water. I found it to produce quite nicely on my favorite desert lakes.

I use this pattern mostly as a search fly, at times when there are no hatches, or when things are particularly slow. It doesn't really imitate any particular insect, but it certainly looks "buggy" when in the water.

Midge Pupa

Hook: TMC 100, size no. 20 to no. 26
Body: Black thread, 6/0
Head/thorax: Black ostrich herl

Tying Steps

Step 1: Form a body of black thread tapering slightly larger towards the head.

Step 2: Tie in one piece of ostrich herl and wind two turns.

Step 3: Finish a small head and cement to complete the Midge Pupa.

Sometimes when things are incredibly difficult, fishing tiny midges is the only answer. This is especially true during the summer doldrum months when fish are picky, the water

is warm, and you are just about to pull your hair out.

Try tiny midge pupae in late evening when fish are feeding, but all other patterns fail. You will lose a significant number of your takes due to hook and tippet size, but when fished on a dry line and 7X tippet, tiny midges, dead drift in the surface film can sometimes make the difference between success or failure.

Night Leech

Hook: Daiichi 2220, size no. 4 or no. 6
Thread: Black
Tail: Black marabou
Body: Black ESTAZ
Wing: Black bunny strip (Zonker style)
Hackle: Black pheasant rump

Tying Steps

Step 1: Tie in a tail of black marabou. Leave a 10-inch piece of black thread at the butt to be used in a later step.

Step 2: Secure a piece of black ESTAZ to the hook and wind forward to form the body.

Step 3: Tie in a 4-inch piece of dyed black rabbit strip at the head of the fly.

Step 4: Pulling the fur forward, with the thread left at the butt of the fly, wind the thread forward securing the rabbit to the top of the body.

Step 5: Tie in a dyed black pheasant rump feather by the tip.

Step 6: Wind the hackle two or three turns and secure. Trim the rabbit strip so that it extends just to the end of the marabou tail. Finish head and cement to complete the Night Leech.

This is the pattern I use most when fishing at night in any lake. I have experimented with several patterns at night and have never found a fly that works as well. Fished on a short line and leader, the Night Leech vibrates and undulates in a seductive manner that no fish can resist.

Dragonfly Nymph

Hook: Daiichi 2441, size no. 6 or no. 8
Thread: Olive
Body: Large olive chenille
Eyes: Commercial mono eyes

Tying Steps

Step 1: Tie in a piece of large olive chenille at the butt of the fly and wind forward 2/3 the way up the hook shank.

Step 2: Tie in a pair of large commercial mono eyes at the head of the fly.

Step 3: Tie in a brown hen hackle or partridge feather by the tip, and then wind the chenille forward working it around and through the eyes.

Step 4: Wind the hackle two turns and secure behind the eyes.

Step 5: Finish head and cement. Also cement the point where you tied the hackle down behind the eyes to complete the Dragonfly Nymph.

Dragonfly nymphs are meat and potatoes to feeding trout in lakes. These hefty insects are a mouthful, and trout are not bashful when they take them. This dragonfly nymph is one of my favorites. It is realistic looking, and very easy to tie.

Fish the dragonfly nymph slowly amongst the bottom weeds. Trout will work the bottom weed beds gorging themselves on these nymphs at times, and the angler who methodically works the weed beds with these giant nymphs awaits some violent and adrenaline-pumping strikes.

Damselfly Nymph

Hook: Daiichi 1270, size no. 10 to no. 14
Thread: Olive
Tail: Olive marabou
Abdomen: Olive dubbing
Ribbing: Gold wire
Thorax: Olive dubbing
Hackle: Olive neck hackle
Eyes: Commercial mono eyes

Tying Steps

Step 1: Tie in a short tail of olive marabou.

Step 2: Tie on a piece of gold wire and then dub on an abdomen of olive dubbing. Wind the wire forward ribbing the abdomen.

Step 3: Tie on a pair of small commercial mono eyes.

Step 4: Secure an olive neck hackle by the tip and then dub on a thorax of olive dubbing.

Step 5: Wind the hackle forward and secure.

Step 6: Wind a little more dubbing around and through the eyes, finish head and cement to complete the Damselfly Nymph.

Damselflies are prolific in lakes. During the time of emergence, those fishing any pattern that resembles these undulating aquatic insects will be in the action.

This is a simple, realistic pattern that is very effective during the emergence as well as at any other time during the summer months. Fish it in an erratic manner to mimic the movements of the naturals.

Chironomid Pupa

Hook: Daiichi 1270, size no. 10 to no. 20
Thread: Black
Abdomen: Black V-RIB
Wingcase: Black Swiss Straw
Thorax: Black dubbing
Gills: White Poly Pro Yarn

Tying Steps

Step 1: Secure a piece of black V-RIB to the hook and wind forward 2/3 the way up the hook shank.

Step 2: Tie in a piece of black Swiss Straw to be used later for the wingcase.

Step 3: Dub on a thorax of black dubbing. Make sure the thorax is at least twice the thickness of the abdomen.

Step 4: Place a small section of Poly Pro Yarn across the top of the hook and secure using a figure eight movement of the tying thread.

Step 5: Pull Swiss Straw forward and secure at head. Trim the Poly Yarn so that it extends out only 1/16 of an inch on each side of the fly. Finish head and cement to complete the Chironomid Pupa.

You simply can't find a lake that doesn't host chironomids. They come in all sizes and colors, but black will get you by most of the time. However, you should have patterns tied in greens, browns, tans and grays, as chironomids are common in these colors also.

There are many chironomid patterns on the market. This is a fairly realistic tie, yet an easy one to produce. It can be fished from the top to the bottom with success.

Floating Chironomid Pupa

Hook: Daiichi 1270, size no. 10 to no. 20
Thread: Black
Tail: Grizzly hackle fibers
Abdomen: Orvis Flexi-Floss
Thorax: Peacock herl

Hackle: Grizzly
Head: Fly Foam

Tying Steps

Step 1: Tie in a tail of grizzly hackle fibers.

Step 2: Secure a piece of Flexi-Floss and a piece of pearl Krystal Flash to the hook.

Step 3: Wind the Flexi-Floss forward and then the ribbing.

Step 4: Cut a small piece of Fly Foam and secure at the head of the fly.

Step 5: Tie in one strand of peacock herl and wind forward. Secure just behind the Fly Foam.

Step 6: Tie in a grizzly neck hackle and wind two turns. Finish head and cement both in front and behind the Fly Foam to complete the Floating Chironomid Pupa.

One of the most difficult aspects of fishing chironomid pupas on the surface is seeing the darn thing when the light is bad. This fly solves that problem with the white Fly Foam that is clearly visible under most conditions.

This pattern is great for imitating the stillborn pupa, or the stage when the adult is separating from the pupal husk. The tail resembles the husk, and the hackle resembles the adult's legs. Cast this fly into an area where fish are visibly working and simply watch for the fly to disappear.

Scud/Freshwater Shrimp

Hook: Daiichi 1150, size no. 10 to no. 16
Thread: Olive
Antennae: Brown calftail hairs and two olive Krystal Flash fibers
Eyes: Commercial mono eyes
Body: Olive dubbing
Shellback: Plastic bag section
Ribbing: Copper wire

Tying Steps

Step 1: Tie in the calftail fibers and two Krystal Flash fibers that extend a little past the calftail.

Step 2: Secure a pair of mono eyes to the hook using a figure eight motion of the tying thread.

Step 3: Cut a piece of plastic Ziploc type bag to a cigar shape and secure to the hook between the eyes. Tie in a piece of copper wire.

Step 4: Dub on a body of olive dubbing. Dub both in front and behind the eyes, tapering down towards

Releasing a nice desert lake brown trout.

A western desert lake in eastern Washington.

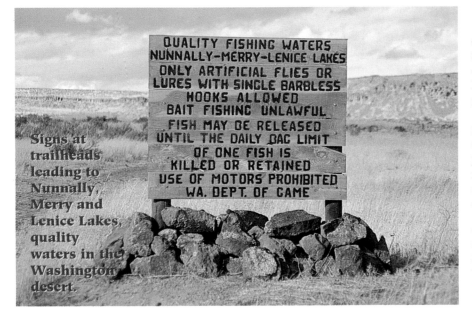

Signs at trailheads leading to Nunnally, Merry and Lenice Lakes, quality waters in the Washington desert.

the eyes, tapering down towards the eye of the hook.

Step 5: Pull plastic forward and secure at the eye of the hook.

Step 6: Wind wire forward and secure.

Step 7: Rough up the dubbing fibers with a bodkin or dubbing teaser. Finish head (tail) and cement to complete the Scud/Freshwater Shrimp.

Freshwater shrimp, or scuds, are found in many desert and high arid lakes. When present, they are staples in the trout's diet. They move erratically, and imitations should be fished in a like manner. Fish this fly around shorelines and structure all through the season.

Stillwater Caddis

Hook: Tiemco 5212, size no. 10 to no. 16
Thread: Tan
Body: Tan dubbing
Hackle: Brown
Wing: Turkey quill

Tying Steps

Step 1: Tie in a quality neck hackle by the tip.

Step 2: Dub on a sparse body using your favorite dubbing material.

Step 3: Palmer the hackle forward and secure.

Step 4: Isolate a small section of turkey quill and secure for the wing. Clip into a "pup tent" shape as shown.

Step 5: Tie in another hackle by the tip and wind two or three turns. Finish head and cement to complete the fly.

Note: For particularly fussy fish, clip the hackle on the bottom side of the fly. This will let it ride low in the surface film, looking a little more realistic.

At times, and on certain waters, the caddis is an important food item to trout. Since the water is not moving in lakes, caddis imitations that more closely resemble the real thing work better than basic, general imitators.

As with most insects, trout will be more interested in the sub-surface stages of caddis. Small, soft hackle flies do a great job of imitating the ascending stage of this insect, but when trout are taking the adults on top those without a realistic caddis pattern will be out of luck.

This is a simple, yet very effective adult caddis pattern. Although the fly shown is tied in tan, it is best to closely match the color of the naturals in the water you are fishing. I usually carry this pattern in shades of browns and oranges to cover all possibilities.

Fishing a chironomid pupa using a strike indicator.

Where to Find Desert & High Arid Lakes

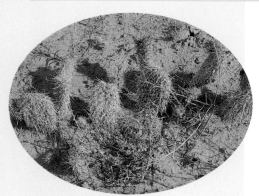

Cactus in the Wyoming desert, be careful not to drop your float tube just anywhere!

Walking into a western desert lake during a rain shower.

While doing research for this book I traveled around ten of our western states in search of desert and high arid lakes. In desert and arid sections of every state I visited, I found lakes. Lakes teeming with trout.

I sampled the fishing in many lakes, and spent a good deal of time talking with the fishermen who frequently fish those waters. My conclusion, after returning from my research trip, was that every western state has this type of trout fishery, and for the most part it is underrated, and sometimes completely overlooked.

As I traveled I found that most waters were basically alike in that they contained the same type of aquatic insects, structure, and the fish demonstrated the same mannerisms. Physical characteristics varied from lake to lake, and types of vegetation varied slightly, but I found that basically a lake is a lake!

It would be impossible to try to list all the desert and high arid lakes available to fishermen across the west. To do so would completely fill a book of this size, and then some. My advice for those seeking out this type of fishery would be to first look at a map. Desert areas are easily identified on most maps. Most quality maps display the larger lakes, but lack when it comes to the detail needed for locating smaller waters.

The DeLorme Map Company produces an Atlas & Gazetteer—a topographical map in book form which shows an entire state in detail. As of this writing not all states are compiled into these Gazetteers, but many are and more are in the works. These books are very handy and can be purchased at most book stores or sporting goods stores.

Probably the best way to find out about the quality lakes in specific areas is to check with local fly shops, but getting those phone numbers is sometimes not the easiest thing to do. Each state's Department of Game, or Department of Fish and Wildlife, or whatever the agency is called, is another very good source. They provide you with information, as well as fishing regulations which will have specific waters listed. You can often spot the best fly fishing waters by their designation in the regulation book. Waters with special regulations like; fly fishing only, selective fishery, etc., are usually the ones to focus your attention on.

However you discover the bountiful desert and high arid lakes found around the west, the effort will be worth it. Some of the best fishing in the country is there for those willing to do a little footwork and seek them out.

Rainbow trout from a western reservoir.

Bibliography

Borger, Gary A., *Naturals*. Harrisburg, Pennsylvania: Stackpole Books, 1980.

Davy, Alfred G., *The Gilly: A Flyfisher's Guide*. Kelowna, B.C. Canada: Alf Davy, 1985.

Cordes, Ron and Randall Kaufmann, *Lake Fishing With a Fly*. Portland, Oregon: Frank Amato Publications, Inc. 1984.

Hafele, Rick and Dave Hughes, *The Complete Book of Western Hatches*. Portland, Oregon: Frank Amato Publications, Inc. 1981.

Merwin, John, *Stillwater Trout*. New York, New York: Nick Lyons Books, 1980.

Raymond, Steve, *Kamloops*. Portland, Oregon: Frank Amato Publications, Inc. 1980, 1994.

Roberts, Donald V., *Fly Fishing Still Waters*. Portland, Oregon: Frank Amato Publications, Inc. 1984.

Shaw, Jack, *Fly Fishing the Trout Lakes*. Mitchell Press Limited, 1976.

Desert wildflowers.

Walking into a lake tucked away in the Washington desert.

LEARN MORE ABOUT FLY FISHING AND FLY TYING WITH THESE BOOKS

If you are unable to find the books shown below at your local book store
or fly shop you can order direct from the publisher below.

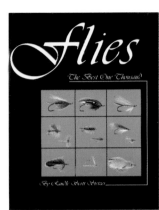

Flies: The Best One Thousand
Randy Stetzer
$24.95

Fly Tying Made Clear and Simple
Skip Morris
$19.95 (HB: $29.95)

The Art of Tying the Dry Fly
Skip Morris
$29.95 (HB: $39.95)

Curtis Creek Manifesto
Sheridan Anderson
$7.95

American Fly Tying Manual
Dave Hughes
$9.95

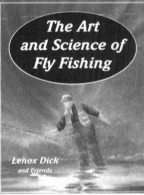

The Art and Science of Fly Fishing
Lenox Dick
$19.95

Western Hatches
Dave Hughes, Rick Hafele
$24.95

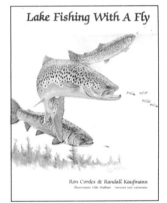

Lake Fishing with a Fly
Ron Cordes, Randall Kaufmann
$26.95

Advanced Fly Fishing for Steelhead
Deke Meyer
$24.95

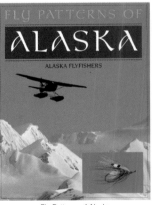

Fly Patterns of Alaska
Alaska Flyfishers
$19.95

Fly Tying & Fishing for Panfish and Bass
Tom Keith
$19.95

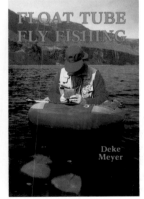

Float Tube Fly Fishing
Deke Meyer
$11.95

VISA, MASTERCARD or AMERICAN EXPRESS ORDERS CALL TOLL FREE: 1-800-541-9498
(9-5 Pacific Standard Time)

Or Send Check or money order to:

*Frank Amato Publications
Box 82112
Portland, Oregon 97282*

(Please add $3.00 for shipping and handling)